MW01487847

TALES FROM THE
LOS ANGELES KINGS
LOCKER ROOM

TALES FROM THE
LOS ANGELES KINGS
LOCKER ROOM

A COLLECTION OF THE GREATEST
KINGS STORIES EVER TOLD

BY
BOB MILLER

SPORTS
PUBLISHING

CONTENTS

ACKNOWLEDGMENTS

The Stanley Cup edition of this book is dedicated to the loyal, passionate Kings fans who finally, after 45 years, saw their dream come true. All of us shared their joy, their excitement and their tears as the Stanley Cup was presented at center ice at Staples Center.

To everyone in the Los Angeles Kings organization, both past and present who devoted so much to this accomplishment; the owners, management, coaches, players, trainers, publicity and communications departments and others who worked so hard, sometimes anonymously, to achieve this goal.

To my friend Randy Schultz, who initiated the process for publication of my first book, *Tales from the Los Angeles Kings*, in 2006.

To *Los Angeles Daily News* sportswriter Tom Hoffarth for his help in getting this book published, to my son Kevin for his computer expertise, to our talented Fox Sports West television crew, my "on-air" partners Jim Fox and Patrick O'Neal, Producer Steve "Hoover" Dorfman, Director Mike Hassan, Stage Manager Donna Moskal, Statistician Doug Mann and to the entire camera, videotape, and audio crew who help make our telecast one of the best in the NHL.

To all my "on-air" partners through the years for their help and cooperation as we enjoyed the peaks and valleys of this franchise.

To my wife of 50 years, Judy, who hardly ever misses a game or telecast, for her love, encouragement and companionship.

To our children, Kristin and Kevin, who began following the Kings when they were 7 and 5 years old and are now adults, who celebrated with us during and after this momentous victory.

To our son-in-law Gilbert and grandchildren, Kaden and Brennon, who also enjoyed their time with this most famous of all sports trophies.

To Niels Aaboe, Senior Editor at Skyhorse Publishing, Inc., for making the update of this book a reality. Thanks to Julie Ganz of

Skyhorse Publishing for her editing skills. It was a pleasure to work with both of you.

—B.M.

PREFACE

I hope you enjoy this Stanley Cup edition of *Tales From the Los Angeles Kings.*

I wanted to write these stories so we can all have a printed record of the most thrilling postseason in Kings history. I'm sure as some of you read the stories, memories will come flooding back as to where you were and what you were doing, whether at the games in person or watching on TV or listening on radio and cheering, screaming and crying right along with thousands of Kings fans as this long awaited moment became reality.

Following the Stanley Cup stories, you will find other stories which were not available when the first book was printed. After that you can read once again, or for the first time, some of the incidents which have taken place down through the years. Not all of the stories printed in the first book are repeated here.

I know all of us will forever remember when the final horn sounded and the Kings became STANLEY CUP CHAMPIONS.

Enjoy!
Bob Miller
2012

Bob Miller

CHAPTER ONE

2012 STANLEY CUP

THE DROUGHT IS OVER

The date was Monday, June 11, 2012 and as the final 3 minutes and 30 seconds ticked away, 18,858 Kings fans were cheering wildly at Staples Center in Los Angeles as the L.A. Kings led the New Jersey Devils 6-1 in Game Six of the National Hockey League Stanley Cup Final. At that point, it was inevitable that the team's 45-year drought would be over and the Kings would win their first-ever Stanley Cup Championship.

As the final horn sounded, there were hugs and tears of joy among Kings fans, most of whom thought they might never see this happen. The Kings won the series four games to two.

My TV partner, Jim Fox, and I recorded the game for a DVD because due to rights held by NBC we were not allowed to televise the game live. Seconds before the game ended I said, "This is for you Kings fans, wherever you may be. The frustration and disappointment of the past is gone. The 45-year drought is over. The Los Angeles Kings are indeed the Kings of the National Hockey League, the 2012 STANLEY CUP CHAMPIONS".

On his Kings radio broadcast, Nick Nickson closed the final seconds by saying, "The Kings have earned their crown, they are the 2012 Stanley Cup Champions."

Then the celebration began with the presentation of the Conn Smythe Trophy to Kings

goalie Jonathan Quick, voted Most Valuable Player of the playoffs, and then the moment Kings fans had waited so long to see, the presentation of the Stanley Cup from NHL Commissioner Gary Bettman to Kings captain Dustin Brown. The Cup was then handed off to each member of the team to the wild applause from the fans.

Fox and I were at our TV location on a balcony outside STAPLES Center to do a postgame show and we were filled with emotion as we looked down on the fans celebrating the title. I was so proud of Kings fans who behaved responsibly and showed the world that you can celebrate a championship without vandalism or rioting.

I finally got into the Kings locker room and promptly got sprayed in the face with champagne, which stung so much I couldn't open my eyes. The players were yelling and screaming and then several of them said, "Bob, you need a drink from the Cup." I couldn't open my eyes so the players lifted the cup to my lips and while I got some champagne in my mouth most of it went down the front of my shirt, tie and suit, but who cared, it was a moment I had been waiting for in 39 years with the team.

After the celebration continued in the arena restaurant, my wife Judy and I got home at 2:30 AM. The next morning we woke and said to each other, "Did that really happen, did we see the Kings win the Stanley Cup?" The celebrations with the Cup were just beginning.

THE UNEXPECTED

You could say that the Kings' run to the Stanley Cup Championship came out of nowhere. At the start of the 2011-12 season, many of the so-called hockey experts predicted the Kings would be contenders for the Cup. But, as the season progressed, the team wasn't living up to the predictions. They had good defense and outstanding goaltending, but their offense was in the doldrums, they couldn't score more than one or two goals a game, and many nights they struggled on the power play.

In December, the Kings management made a decision—a coaching change had to be made. On December 11, 2011, head coach Terry Murray was relieved of his duties and assistant coach John Stevens was named interim and coached the Kings for four games. At the time, the Kings were in 12th place in the 15-team Western Conference and were last in the NHL in goals, averaging just 2.24 per game.

Kings General Manager Dean Lombardi had one man in mind to take over, and on December 20th the Kings named Darryl Sutter as the new head coach. Sutter had played eight years for the Chicago Blackhawks and also coached Chicago, San Jose and Calgary and had worked with Lombardi in San Jose. He was very happy working on his huge farm in Alberta, but he accepted the Kings' challenge and coached his first Kings game on December 22nd, a 3-2 victory over the Anaheim Ducks at Staples Center in L.A.

The Kings responded well to Sutter, who gave them more leeway offensively but still kept the defensive structure in place. The Kings were unbeaten in regulation in their first eight games under Sutter and lost only once in regulation in their first 15 games under his leadership.

Still, the Kings looked as if they might miss the playoffs altogether as the regular season wound down. The race was so tight that the Kings could win their Division and finish third in the West, or could also drop to 7th or 8th or be out entirely. With two games left in the season, the Kings were in first place in the Pacific and 3rd in the Western Conference. Had they finished in those spots, they would have had home ice advantage to open the playoffs. However, they lost the final two games to San Jose and dropped to third in the Division but made the playoffs by securing the 8th and final spot in the Western Conference.

In one of those losses to San Jose, on April 5th at STAPLES Center, we saw something that none of us had ever seen before. Late in the third period, the Sharks' Ryane Clowe, while on the bench, reached over the boards with his stick and poked the puck off the stick of the Kings' Jarret Stoll, breaking up a Kings 2 on 1 rush. None of the referees or linesmen saw the illegal play, so no penalty was called. San Jose won the game in overtime, but the Kings still clinched the final playoff berth that night when Dallas lost to Nashville.

In my opinion, it was incredible that the NHL made no statement about such an illegal play, nor did Clowe receive even so much as a reprimand.

Then the improbable Kings' run to the championship began.

THE RUN TO THE CUP

By gaining the 8th and last playoff spot in the Western Conference, the Kings' "reward" was to face the number-one team in the NHL in the regular season, the Vancouver Canucks. Vancouver finished with 111 points, more than any team in the league and 16 points more than the Kings. Aside from Kings management, coaches, and players, few people gave the Kings much of a chance against the potent Canucks, who tied for the fourth-most goals in the regular season.

The series opened in Vancouver with most Kings fans hoping the Kings could win the series and advance to the second round for the first time in 11 years. To the dismay of overconfident Vancouver fans, the Kings won the first two games of the series 4-2 in each game. In my opinion, this is what gave the Kings the confidence to believe they could play with and beat anybody they met in the entire playoffs.

Kings captain Dustin Brown, a quiet individual off the ice, stepped up and provided the on-ice leadership the Kings needed. He scored two short-handed goals in Game Two to tie an NHL playoff record, and for only the third time in the Kings' 45-year history, they won the first two games of a playoff series. It was also only the third time Kings players had scored two short-handed goals in one playoff game. Mike Murphy and Andre St. Laurent did it on April 9, 1980 vs. the New York Islanders, and Jari Kurri and Dave Taylor did it on May 21, 1993 vs. Toronto.

The series then shifted to Los Angeles, and the Kings won 1-0 as goalie Jonathan Quick faced 41 shots in recording the shutout and Dustin Brown scored the only goal. In the second period, Brown further displayed his leadership with a thundering legal body check on the Canucks' leading scorer Henrik Sedin, and for the first time in team history the Kings had a three-games-to-none lead in a playoff series. Kings fans were primed for the team to sweep the Canucks in Game Four, which would have been the first time in NHL history that a #8 seeded team swept the regular season first-place team.

It wasn't to be, however, as the Canucks (who fell behind 1-0) came back to win the game 3-1 and send the series back to Vancouver. Many thought this was the "foot in the door" the Canucks needed to get back in the series. Game Five was a low-scoring, hard-fought battle. The Kings tied the score in the third period on a goal by Brad Richardson and then won it in overtime when Jarrett Stoll scored to give the Kings the 2-1 victory and eliminate Vancouver. It was only the 10th time in league history that an 8th-seeded team eliminated the #1 seed, and only the 6th time that the President's Trophy winner had been eliminated in the first round.

Next up for the Kings was a series against the third-place team, in the regular season the St. Louis Blues. The Blues had also changed coaches during the season, after only 13 games when they named Ken Hitchcock as head coach. Hitchcock, who was voted NHL Coach of the Year, led the Blues to the second seed in the West and tied for the fourth-most wins in the league, with 49. The series pitted the top two defensive teams in the regular season, St. Louis first with a goals against average of 1.86 and the Kings second with an average of 2.03. It also featured the top two goalies in the NHL, Brian Elliott of St. Louis and Jonathan Quick of the Kings. Elliott also led in save percentage and Quick led in shutouts with 10, so it figured to be a low-scoring, defensive series.

The Kings had other thoughts in mind. In Game One in St. Louis in front of 19,391 Blues fans, the Kings continued their shorthanded onslaught. Low-scoring defenseman Matt Greene scored shorthanded in the second period for what proved to be the game-winning goal in a 3-1 Kings victory.

Because of the demand for press credentials, the normal press box was extended to provide seats for people such as myself and Jim Fox who were doing postgame TV shows. I know you've heard about "no cheering or booing in the press box," but at times when you are not "on the air," it's hard to control yourself. Whenever the Kings would score, I would find myself jumping to my feet, pumping my arms and cheering, but not too loudly. Jim Fox, on the other hand, as a former Kings player, was more demonstrative, especially regarding referees calls. On some penalties called against the Kings, Jim would jump up, wave his arms and scream at the referee, "You can't make that call," or "that's the wrong call," etc. He really gets wrapped up in the game, and his professional athlete's competitiveness comes out. At least we didn't get kicked out.

The Blues were desperate to tie the series in Game Two, but again the Kings surprised everyone. In the first period, the Kings scored four goals, including two by Anze Kopitar, one of which was another shorthanded tally. The Blues were demoralized losing 5-2, and the Kings again had a two-games-to-none lead headed back home. In Game Three at STAPLES Center, the Kings jumped out to a 3-1 lead on their way to a 4-2 win and a three-games-to-none lead, to the delight of another overflow crowd of over 18,000.

Kings fans were pumped for Game Four and showed up with brooms, indicating a four-game sweep was on their minds. The Kings didn't disappoint them. With the game tied 1-1, Dustin Brown scored the final two goals, the last one into an empty net, and the crowd was in a frenzy in the closing seconds. It was the first four-game sweep of a seven-game series in Kings history. The Kings had now played nine playoff games and had a record of 8-1. They became only the fourth team in the last 16 years to win eight of nine playoff games.

Now the Kings had time to rest until the Nashville-Phoenix series was concluded, and the Kings would find out who their opponent would be in the Western Conference Final.

The Phoenix Coyotes eliminated Nashville in a mild upset, and once again the Kings would open the next series on the road. The Kings knew they were for real by now, and in the eyes of most fans, Coyote fans included, the Kings dominated the two games on the Coyotes' home ice, winning 4-2 and 4-0.

It takes total teamwork to play the way the Kings were in these playoffs. That was indicated by the play of two rookies playing in their first NHL playoffs. During the regular season, the Kings recalled forwards Dwight King and Jordan Nolan, who fit right in.

In fact, at one point King scored 5 goals in 5 games, and both players brought size and strength to the Kings lineup. In Game Two, a 4-0 shutout, King scored again, and Jeff Carter, a mid-season trade acquisition from Columbus, scored the three-goal hat trick. During that physical game, Shane Doan and Martin Hanzal of Phoenix were given five-minute major penalties and game misconducts, Doan for boarding Trevor Lewis and Hanzal for boarding Dustin Brown. Hanzal was later given a one-game suspension by the NHL for his dangerous play.

At that point, the Kings had won seven straight playoff games, a club record, and had tied a NHL record with seven straight road wins in one playoff year. Quick had also tied a Kings record with his 3rd career playoff shutout, stopping 24 Phoenix shots, and set a Kings record with three shutouts in one playoff year. For the third consecutive series, the Kings had taken a two-games-to-none lead.

I think most fans feel that the atmosphere on the team plane after a win is loud and boisterous. That is definitely not the case. On the way home from Phoenix, the Kings were not celebrating; they knew they needed two more wins in this series. Helping that demeanor, I believe, is the body language of coach Sutter. While previous coach Terry

Murray would remain in his seat for most of the flights, watching game tapes on his computer, Darryl Sutter is much more restless. He is constantly up out of his seat, pacing the aisle and staring toward the rear of the plane where the players sit. I always get the feeling the players are wondering, "Is he looking at me?" or "What is he looking for and what is going through his mind?".

By now the Kings were gaining momentum and notoriety in hockey circles. Where had this outstanding play come from, since the regular season held no promise of this type of dominance? Another overflow crowd jammed Staples Center on May 17th for Game Three. The Kings fell behind, but Kopitar and once again Dwight King each scored their 5th goals of the series, and the Kings won 2-1 and for the third straight series led three games to none.

The fans were poised for another Kings sweep in Game Four, but Phoenix goalie Mike Smith shut out the Kings, and captain Shane Doan contributed two goals as the Coyotes staved off elimination with a 2-0 win.

Phoenix fans felt they had a chance to get back in the series at home, and they were in a frenzy as the Coyotes led by scores of 1-0 and 2-1. Kopitar had scored another shorthanded goal for the Kings to tie the game at one. The Kings fell behind again before Drew Doughty and Brad Richardson scored for the Kings to give them a 3-2 lead. Nevertheless, defenseman Keith Yandle tied the game for Phoenix late in the second period. The game went into overtime, and the Phoenix crowd was incensed when Dustin Brown leveled Michal Rozsival with a huge hit just inside the Phoenix blue line and it appeared as if Rozsival was severly injured. No penalty was called on the play, which further upset the crowd. It was later revealed that Rozsival had received a charley horse and not a severe knee injury as was first thought. To literally add insult to injury, the Kings' Dustin Penner scored the game-winning and series-deciding goal about 12 seconds after the hit by Brown.

Jim Fox and I were in our postgame TV location, which was right in the stands with Coyote fans all around us, when the Kings won. During overtime, those fans knew we were with the Kings, and they were screaming at us and the referees, "They never call anything on Brown, he can do whatever he wants." It could have turned into an ugly scene, but thankfully it didn't.

Not so on the ice, as the Kings celebrated and the Coyotes were visibly upset during the traditional handshake line, which is the greatest show of sportsmanship in any sport.

Words were exchanged at that time by Doan and Hanzal, directed at Brown.

Reportedly Hanzal, who was the only player suspended for a game in the series, said to Brown, "I'll go through with this tradition, but you are on my list the first time we meet next season." Shane Doan and goalie Mike Smith, who had deliberately chopped Brown from behind across the back of the knees with his goal stick, both received game misconducts at the end of the game for throwing their sticks along the ice toward the referees.

It didn't matter—the Coyotes' season was over and the Kings were moving on.

I mentioned before that there had been no celebrating by the Kings after winning the previous series. This victory gave the Kings the Western Conference Championship and a trip to the Stanley Cup Final, so they allowed themselves a moment to celebrate. Near the team bus, General Manager Dean Lombardi, Assistant General Manager Ron Hextall, the coaches, trainers, broadcasters, and other team personnel exchanged handshakes, and then it was time to prepare for the next opponent in the Stanley Cup Final.

Upon arriving back at a private terminal at Los Angeles International airport, the team was informed that about 4,000 Kings fans were lining the road outside of the parking lot.

Everyone was told not to stop and sign autographs because that would cause a traffic jam, but it was a wild scene as we drove past the fans all dressed in Kings jerseys, jackets,

and sweatsuits, screaming and hollering and reaching out to touch the players. It was the first time in 19 years that the Kings had been to the Final, and these fans had waited a long time to celebrate.

But the best was yet to come.

STANLEY CUP FINAL

Kings fans had waited 19 years to see their team in the Stanley Cup Final. The last time it happened was 1993 when the Kings lost in five games to Montreal. (You can read about that series elsewhere in this book).

The Kings had to wait eight days to find out who their opponent would be in their quest for the Stanley Cup. It took that long for the Eastern Conference Final between the New Jersey Devils and the New York Rangers to be decided. The Devils won the series 4 games to 2.

For the fourth straight series, the Kings would open on the road, but so far that had been no problem as the Kings at this point had set an NHL record with eight straight road wins. Some felt the Devils would be a tougher test for the Kings than the Rangers. I was happy it was New Jersey for two reasons— I'm not fond of New York and I also thought it would help the Kings focus if they were staying in New Jersey rather than having to deal with all the distractions in Manhattan.

The first two games in New Jersey were typical low-scoring defensive-minded games, which featured two goalies at opposite ends of their careers. The Kings' Jonathan Quick was a 26 year old who had played in only 12 NHL playoff games prior to this season. For New Jersey, 40 year old Martin Brodeur, who had already won three Stanley Cups in his career and is destined for the Hall of Fame, was goaltending.

One of the strengths of the Kings in these playoffs was balanced scoring and offensive contributions from a variety of players. Evidence of that came in Game One, when Colin Fraser, who had only 2 goals in 67 regular season games, scored the first goal of the game, his first-ever playoff goal in the NHL. A goal by Anton Volchenkov with 1:12 left in the second period tied the score, and that's the way regulation ended before the teams went to sudden death overtime. At 8:13 into overtime, the Kings' Justin Williams flipped the puck to an open ice area in the Devils zone, where Anze Kopitar swooped in on a breakaway and beat Brodeur for the game-wining goal. The Kings had now won nine straight road playoff games.

Game Two was almost a carbon copy of Game One. The Kings again scored first, when young defenseman Drew Doughty stunned the crowd with a spectacular goal, going almost end to end unassisted for a 1-0 first period lead.

Again the Devils came back and tied the score early in the third period to once again send the game into overtime. Jeff Carter, who foiled on his first attempt to score, regained the puck, circled behind the net, came back out in front, and beat Brodeur to the stick side to win the game 2-1 at 13:42 of the extra period. Now the Kings were heading home with 10 straight road wins and a 2-games-to-none lead in the series.

On June 4th, 18,764 spectators, an all-time STAPLES Center attendance record for hockey, were giddy with excitement to witness only the 2nd home ice Stanley Cup Final in Kings history. They were not disappointed as the Kings, after a scoreless first period, scored twice in the second and twice again in the third period to win the game 4-0. Quick made 22 saves for his team-record third shutout of the playoffs, and at this point the Kings had incredibly led every playoff series three games to none.

Another all-time Staples Center hockey record attendance of 18,867 jammed the building on June 6th, most of whom were extremely confident that the Kings would sweep the series and win their first ever Stanley Cup. How confident or over-confident were they? Here's an example:

I had to be in the Staples Center area about noon that day for some TV and radio appearances. Thousands of Kings fans were already there dressed in their Kings colors even though the game was not scheduled to start until 5 p.m. They were hollering to me, "Bob, tonight's the night, we'll win the cup tonight" and "We're going to sweep the series tonight." Perhaps the biggest display of over-confidence came about half an hour before the game. My TV partner, Jim Fox, and I recorded a preview of each game, which is played on the arena scoreboard just before the start of each game. We recorded it in the Zamboni tunnel, and while I was there early a Kings fan leaned over a railing and said, "Bob, can I get a picture of your ring?" I have a Hockey Hall of Fame ring from my induction in 2000. I said sure and held the ring up for the photo. Just then, another Kings fan came running over and asked "Have the Kings gotten their rings already?", meaning of course the Stanley Cup rings. Yeah sure, with only three wins the Kings have already passed out the rings, but that's how sure the fans were that the Cup would be presented that night.

I believe most fans aren't aware of the competitive attitude of professional athletes. In spite of losing the previous game 4-0, and being down three games to none, the Devils were not about to roll over and let the Kings win, and they didn't. The Devils won 3-1, to the disappointment of the Kings crowd, and the Devils were still alive as we headed back to Jersey.

PRESSURE MOUNTS

Every team wants to win the Stanley Cup on their home ice and celebrate along with their fans. On the other hand, you want to win it whenever and wherever you get the chance, and the Kings had another chance in Game 5 in New Jersey.

Since that could be a Cup-clinching game, Kings management was gracious enough to invite players' wives and families along with the wives of other team personnel to fly on a chartered flight to the East Coast. My wife, Judy, was included and she said the group was treated in a first-class manner. They were housed at a hotel in Manhattan but were not in contact with the players or other team members who were housed in New Jersey. The group was treated to two suites in the Prudential Center, home of the Devils, to watch the game.

In the first period, Kings goalie Quick made one of his few mistakes. Coming out of the net to play the puck, he mishandled it and was slow getting back into position and Zach Parise took advantage to give the Devils a 1-0 first period lead. Justin Williams tied the score for the Kings in the second period, but just under six minutes later in that period Bryce Salvador fired a shot that glanced off Kings defenseman Slava Voynov into the net for what proved to be the game-winning goal. New Jersey now had confidence and momentum trailing the series three games to two, and they felt they had the Kings nervous about perhaps blowing a three-games-to-none lead which had only been done twice before in NHL history. The Kings' NHL record 10-game road winning streak had ended, and so had this chance to skate with the Cup.

As the Kings' wives waited outside the arena for the bus to take them to the airport for the flight home, Devils fans taunted them by giving the "choke" sign, and chanting "Go back to Hollywood, you chokers," as well as some other profanity-laced comments.

As the Kings' team bus left for the airport, Devils fans also put their hands to their necks in a "choke" sign indicating that the Kings couldn't handle the pressure.

KINGS OF THE NHL

Whereas before Game Four Kings fans were extremely over-confident the Kings would win, now there was a ripple of nervousness among the crowd with comments like, "Do you think we can win tonight?" No one wanted to tempt fate with a final and deciding Game Seven back in New Jersey.

Hindsight is easy, but in looking back at the start of the game, I thought the Kings' play impressed upon the Devils that, "You are NOT going to win in our building tonight."

Still, it took one of the most deciding penalties in Stanley Cup Final history to set the tone of the game. Ten minutes in to a scoreless first period, the Devils' forward Steve Bernier slammed Kings defenseman Rob Scuderi face-first into the boards from behind. Bernier (no relation to the Kings' backup goalie Jonathan Bernier) received a five-minute major penalty and was tossed out of the game. Scuderi went to the Kings' dressing room for repairs. The doctor who tended to him told me days later at a party that he put 37 stitches in Rob's upper lip and up toward his nose. In keeping with NHL directives about detecting a concussion, the doctor told Scuderi he would have to ask him a few questions to see how he reacted. Rob said to the doctor, "Don't you even think about not putting me back in that game." The doctor proceeded to ask Rob what day it was and Rob's answer was "It's the day of destiny," and the doctor said, "Get back out there."

Meanwhile, the Kings' power play, which had struggled for most of the season, took advantage of this opportunity. The Kings took control of the game, scoring three times on the major power play as Dustin Brown, Jeff Carter and Trevor Lewis gave the Kings a 3-0 lead at the end of the first period to the delight of the roaring crowd.

Just over a minute in to the second period, Jeff Carter scored again, his 8th goal of the playoffs, and the Kings led 4-0. Driving to the game that day I thought to myself, "I wish we could get out to a 4-0 lead and just relax." Well, we had the 4-0 lead, but I still couldn't relax because there was too much time remaining in the game. Even though the crowd thought it was "over," at this point I got a little nervous when the Devils scored and then with 17 seconds left in the period Dustin Penner took a roughing penalty and the Devils had the man advantage. That penalty carried over into the 3rd period and I thought, "Wow, if they score here it will be 4-2 with about 18 minutes left. If they then get another goal it'll be 4-3 and it will really be nervous time."

As the third period progressed, the desperate Devils pulled their goalie for an extra attacker with about 4:30 left. Trevor Lewis scored into the empty net for a 5-1 Kings lead, and the crowd knew the Stanley Cup would belong to the Kings. Fifteen seconds after that goal, with the crowd still in a frenzy, Matt Greene scored for the Kings to make it 6-1. I felt it was so great that the Kings won in a rout so the outcome was not in doubt and the fans had the final several minutes to celebrate and roar their approval. The tears of joy were flowing not only in the stands, but also in our broadcast location as I looked at my partner Jim Fox, and he couldn't hold back the tears. Jim had played ten years for the Kings, is still 8th in Kings all-time scoring and has devoted years to the organization previously in the role of Director of Community Relations and at this point for 22 years as the analyst on our Kings telecasts. In keeping with hockey tradition that if you are a player or ex-player, you don't touch the Cup until you win it, I don't believe Jim had ever broken that tradition. Now he had that opportunity, so he had the right to shed a few tears. Players are extremely superstitious, so earlier in the game when the Kings had a 4-0 lead, the crowd was chanting "We want the Cup" in our broadcast location, Jim was waving his arms indicating for them to stop the chant because the game was far from over. After the Kings' 5th goal the chant became "We've Got the Cup," and now Jim agreed.

Personally, I felt such elation and pride as I watched the Stanley Cup handed to Captain Dustin Brown. Many fans told me they were happy most of all for me because I had experienced 39 years with the team at that point, and though I appreciated the sentiment, I was happy not only for the players and everyone in the Kings organization, but also for all the loyal Kings fans who had spent over 45 years waiting for this moment.

Now it was time to organize the parade and numerous additional celebrations.

PARADE AND RALLY

Three days after the Kings won the Stanley Cup, thousands more fans got to join in the celebration. An estimated 250,000 fans lined both sides of the parade route on Figueroa Street, which runs past STAPLES Center. Kings players and other team personnel were riding in open air, double-decker busses. As the busses traveled to the starting point of the parade, they had to travel a short distance on the 110 Freeway in downtown Los Angeles, and it was quite a sight to see passengers in cars hanging out of their windows taking pictures of the busses and cheering while the drivers honked their horns.

When the parade turned the corner onto Figueroa, we were astounded to see the thousands of people lining the sidewalks, and parking structures, waving and cheering out of open office windows. When the procession turned in front of STAPLES Center, a huge torrent of

confetti rained down on a flatbed truck carrying Kings captain Dustin Brown, alternate captains Anze Kopitar and Matt Greene, and the Stanley Cup.

Following the parade, a rally was held inside STAPLES Center with 19,000 fans who were able to obtain the free tickets in attendance. The entire team, as well as team management personnel, was introduced to the continuous ovation from the crowd.

Stanley Cup parade at Staples Center. *PHOTO BY BOB MILLER*

CUP RECEPTION

One of the great traditions in hockey is that each player on the winning team gets a day with the Cup to celebrate with family and friends. Owners, coaches, trainers, and in the Kings' case, the radio and TV broadcasters also received time with the trophy. It is the only professional trophy I know of that is shared with the fans, and that makes it unique. My wife and I were offered our time with the Cup on June 26th from 8 p.m. to midnight. Our plan was to have a reception at our house, but when the invitation list reached 90 we decided we needed more room. We had only a few days to organize the party, so we rented space at a Country Club near our home. The list of 90 ended up with 180 people attending. since when we invited someone they would call the next day and ask if their mom and dad and brother and sister and kids could attend.

One of the great joys for me was to see the looks on the faces of people who get their first glimpse, in person, at the Stanley Cup. They would ask me, "Can I touch it ?", "Can I kiss it?" and I would say "Yes, you can kiss it and we've giving free tetanus shots in the back of the room."

I'm not sure which has more DNA on it, the Stanley Cup or the Blarney Stone in Ireland, and I've kissed both.

Among those invited was our UPS delivery man, Robert Fredericks. He is such a huge Kings fan that many times he stops at my house, even without a delivery, just to talk about a Kings game. He displayed some imagination and humor when he showed up in a Kings jersey with a number 12 on the back, signifying 2012, and where a player's name is positioned he had the word FINALLY. I joked, "That's what I say when my package arrives."

Judy and I had already attended several Cup parties, and on the way home I asked, "Are we going to go to every Stanley Cup party? We paused just a few seconds and then said, "Yes, we

Bob and wife Judy with Stanley Cup. *PHOTO BY KEVIN MILLER*

ARE going to go to every party." Who knows when or if we may ever have this opportunity again?

In late July we attended Jim Fox's party with the Cup. Also attending that party was Kings assistant coach Jamie Kompon, whose name will be engraved on the Cup. The Cup rule is that only someone whose name is on the cup can lift it for someone to take a drink. Jamie spent most of the night pouring various liquids into the mouths of guests, including Judy and myself.

A chaperone or custodian from the Hockey Hall of Fame always accompanies the Cup to its destination. You fill out a form, which includes the date and hours you will have the Cup, the address where it is to be delivered and the warning, "The Cup will be picked up and taken away early if it is not treated with respect."

Another great tradition of the Cup is that the names of players, coaches, general managers and some others appear on the Cup. There are five levels of rings and when the bottom ring is filled, the top ring is taken off and sent to the Hall of Fame and a new blank ring is placed on the bottom. The Kings names will be on the Cup for 57 years before that ring is placed in the Hall of Fame.

2

PRESEASON

THERE USED TO BE AN ARENA

LOCKED OUT

The Stanley Cup Champion Los Angeles Kings were ready to open the 2012-13 season on October 12, 2012, at which time they would raise the Stanley Cup banner to the rafters at the Staples Center and hand out the championship rings in front of over 18 thousand screaming fans. Unfortunately, that did not happen due to a collective bargaining agreement between the owners and players that expired on September 15th.

Since no new agreement was in place, the NHL owners locked out the players, and the season did not start on time. This was tremendously disappointing to Kings and hockey fans across the U.S. and Canada, and for the Kings all the momentum of winning the Cup in June was lost.

LA Kings Insider Rich Hammond, who did such a great job covering the team for the Kings website, decided to take a job with the Orange County Register covering USC football and basketball. That left a huge void on the Kings website, and I was asked to write some stories so fans could still read about hockey each day.

Our former television producer, Bob Borgen, suggested I write about arenas in which I broadcast Kings hockey, that no longer exist, either having been demolished or which no longer are used for NHL hockey.

I have stories about several of those arenas and with apologies to the Frank Sinatra song, "There Used to Be A Ballpark," I included those stories in this next chapter, called "There Used to Be an Arena." I thought I would write some thoughts about NHL arenas which no longer exist or no longer have hockey but where I broadcast Kings' games during my 40 years with the team. I was shocked when I started making out a list and found there are 29 of those former arenas. In fact, the only ones I have ever broadcast in that are still standing for hockey are: Madison Square Garden, New York Rangers; Nassau County Veterans Memorial Coliseum, the N.Y. Islanders; Rexall Place in Edmonton, the Oilers; Honda Center in Anaheim, the Ducks; Nationwide Arena in Columbus, the Blue Jackets; and Bridgestone Arena in Nashville, the Predators.

CHICAGO STADIUM

This arena is the most nostalgic for me, since I grew up in Chicago and as a youngster, around 1950, my mother used to take me and my best friend Joe March to the Stadium to watch the Blackhawks. The Hawks were not very good in those years, so we could arrive about 10 minutes before game time and sit anywhere in the house. The Stadium was built for $9.5 million (in today's dollars that would be $129 million) in 1928. It opened on March 28, 1929, and the first Blackhawks game was played there on December 15 of that year. The Stadium was the home of the Blackhawks until the final game was played there on April 28, 1994, when the Hawks lost a playoff game to Toronto by a score of 1-0. At the time it was built, it was the largest sports arena in the world.

Having seen my first NHL game in that arena, it was always a thrill for me to broadcast a game there as the L.A. Kings announcer. Here are some of the things I remember about the loudest stadium in the NHL.

- The smell of hot dogs and sausages cooking at the concession stands as you entered, as well as the smell of stale beer.

- The sound of the Barton organ, the largest theatre organ in North America. Played for years by Al Melgard, the organ had 3,363 pipes and had a volume of a military band of 2,500 pieces. When the organ started, our radio broadcast booth located on the third level would actually shake.

- The atmosphere in the building during the playing and singing of the National Anthem. At the first note, the crowd would start roaring and increase the roar with each measure until, by the end of the song, the entire building was in a frenzy before the game had even started. For the Blackhawks, it was a tremendous boost, and for the opposing players it was the most intimidating situation in the entire NHL.

- The crowd noise, because those old buildings were not acoustically perfect as arenas are today. The sound would bounce off brick and steel.

- The irregular size of the rink. It was 185 feet long—15 feet short of regulation.

- The dressing rooms, both those of the Hawks and those of the visitors, were located in the basement underneath the ice, and the teams had to climb 22 stairs to get to the ice surface.

- The Blackhawks theme song. As soon as the organist saw the Hawks goalie reach the playing surface, he would start a stirring rendition of "Here Come the Hawks."

- The world's worst scoreboard. It wasn't digital like you see today— it had dials and sweep second hands all over it, lit by different colors. It was so impossible to read that even Blackhawks players would have to give hand signals to their coach to let him know how much time was left in a penalty. For announcers, all you could do was guess at the time remaining.

- The neighborhood on West Madison Street, which was one of the worst in the city. My friend, Joe, would wait for me to finish my postgame show and then drive me to the hotel. One night as we walked to his car, another car drove up slowly behind us. I was getting nervous and asked him what was going on. He informed me that it was an unmarked Chicago Police car which would follow you to your car, make sure you were inside with the windows rolled up and the engine started. Then they would go and escort other fans to their cars. The neighborhood was so bad that taxi cabs would not even venture in to the area to pick up writers who had to stay late to write their game stories. The Blackhawks PR person would have to give the writers a ride to their hotel. So where did they put the new United Center? Right across the street from the old stadium. The neighborhood has been cleaned up and is a lot better now, or so it seems.

- The great vantage point for our radio and/or TV broadcasts. The stadium was built for hockey, and the steep
seating afforded everyone a fantastic view of the game
with spectators and announcers alike right on top of the
action.

The Chicago Stadium was demolished in 1995. Most everyone you ask will say that the "Madhouse on Madison" was the
greatest hockey arena they ever experienced.

DETROIT OLYMPIA

Another great old hockey arena in which I had a chance to
broadcast Kings' games was the Detroit Olympia. In fact, it was
built two years before the Chicago Stadium and was the model
for the arena in Chicago, so both arenas were similar in design
and had spectacular views for hockey, with the crowd and the
announcers right on top of the action.

The Olympia, nicknamed "The Old Red Barn," was located
just northwest of downtown Detroit at the corner of Grand Riv-
er and McGraw, and not in the greatest of neighborhoods. The
Olympia opened on November 22, 1927 and for 52 years
was the home of Detroit professional hockey teams, starting
with the Detroit Cougars and ending with the Red Wings.

Our broadcast location was one of the best in the NHL. We
had a booth in the upper deck, and we were practically hanging
out over the ice, unlike today in some new arenas where the
press box and broadcast booths are in the highest reaches of the
building.

Musician Glenn Frey, of the Eagles, is from Detroit and a
huge hockey fan. One day he told me he was going to be in
Detroit when the Kings played there, so I asked if he would
be our guest on TV. I told him I would let the press box usher
know he was coming between periods. When the period ended,

he still hadn't shown up and I wondered what happened. Glenn is relatively small in stature, and soon there was a knock on the door of our booth and the usher said, 'There's a guy out here who says he's with the Philadelphia Eagles and I don't believe him.' I convinced him to allow Glenn to join us.

For many of the years I did Kings hockey, the Red Wings were not very good. From 1973-74 to 1982-83, they missed the playoffs nine of 10 years. One particular Kings player who always had success against Detroit was Marcel Dionne, much to the chagrin of Detroit fans. Marcel had started his career as a Red Wing, and the Kings acquired his rights in 1975. Detroit fans thought Marcel was a traitor and came to L.A. only for the money. Every time the Kings would play in the Olympia, Detroit fans would mercilessly boo Dionne and hold up derisive signs aimed at him. One game, Marcel had a hat trick which included his 300th career goal in a 7-3 Kings win, and the crowd got more incensed with each goal.

At the end of the game, my broadcast partner at the time, Pete Weber, went down on the ice to interview Marcel. As the interview started, Red Wing fans started throwing glass bottles from the upper deck. When one crashed close to Pete and Marcel, Pete said on the air, 'This is London,' just as reporters did during the bombing of that city during World War II. Pete quickly decided to end the interview, and he and Marcel got safely off the ice.

The Olympia had a lobby where visiting players could meet their friends and family after the game. That night, no one with the Kings was allowed to go into the lobby, fearing it would not be safe. The Kings bus pulled up to a back door of the locker room and got close enough so that when the bus doors opened, no fans could get between the building and the door, and the Kings got out in a safe manner.

In 1979 the Red Wings moved into their current home, the Joe Louis Arena, where the broadcast location is not nearly as good as it was at the Olympia. In fact, I believe they forgot to put in a press box when the building was built, and it's one of the worst in the NHL.

The Olympia fell into disrepair, and shortly after the Red Wings moved, the wrecking ball demolished everything but the memories of one of the great old hockey arenas.

BOSTON GARDEN

The Boston Garden, home of the Bruins, opened on November 17, 1928, and was demolished in 1997. Located on top of North Station, which was the hub for the Boston and Maine railroad, it cost $10 million to build, and the first team sporting event there was a hockey game on November 20, 1928, which the Montreal Canadiens won 1-0 over the Boston Bruins. 17,000 fans – two thousand over capacity – attended while other fans without tickets broke windows and doors and stormed their way in.

I used to see the Garden on television on the CBS NHL Game of the Week, and I used to think how beautiful it looked. I saw it in person in 1973, when I broadcast University of Wisconsin hockey in the NCAA tournament, and my image was dashed. It was old and filthy, but because it was built for boxing, everyone had a great view of the game and our broadcast location was outstanding. We were located in a platform hanging off the first balcony and were so close to the visiting bench we could hear the players talking to each other.

Some of the quirks of the Garden included the fact that the ice surface was nine feet shorter and two feet narrower than regulation. For that reason, I always seemed to feel like I was racing to keep up with the action on my play-by-play. The teams also didn't sit on the same side of the ice but across from each other, and due to the smaller dimensions, the Bruins always seemed to tailor their teams to take advantage of that size.

The visitors' dressing room was small, hot and with questionable plumbing. There was no air conditioning in the building, and twice in the Stanley Cup Final between the Bruins and the Edmonton Oilers the games were disrupted by power failures. The electrical situation was probably the reason that many nights I would be doing play-by-play on TV with a technician crawling under my legs to make an adjustment.

In spite of the shortcomings, the Garden had a great history of outstanding players and teams. In the modern era, I got to describe the exploits of Bobby Orr, Phil Esposito, Johnny Bucyk, Ken Hodge, and Gerry Cheevers. Boston hockey fans are avid and boisterous and in the '70s liked to say, 'Jesus saves, and Esposito scores on the rebound.'

One of the great playoff series I had the pleasure of broadcasting was in 1976 between the heavily favored Bruins and the Los Angeles Kings. The Bruins shut out the Kings in Game 1, 4-0, but the Kings evened the series by winning Game 2, 3-2, on a goal by Butch Goring 27 seconds into overtime. Game 3 was in Los Angeles and the Kings won, 6-4, led by Marcel Dionne's hat trick – the first of his playoff career – and the goaltending of Rogie Vachon. Boston's Cheevers shut out the Kings, 3-0, to tie the series at two wins apiece heading back to Boston.

Game 5 in the Garden was a disaster for the Kings, who after taking a 1-0 lead gave up the next seven goals and lost 7-1. Game 6 in Los Angeles was a must-win for the Kings. I'll never forget the ovation the Kings got when they took the ice that night, in spite of losing the previous game in Boston. The ovation lasted so long that referee Andy Van Hellemond told the singer to start the anthem or he was going to drop the puck. Unbeknownst to everyone was that Boston's Wayne Cashman had deliberately cut the microphone cord with his skate.

The Kings were behind 3-1 at the end of two periods but scored twice in the third on two goals by Mike Corrigan, the tying goal coming with just 2:12 left in regulation. The longest overtime in Kings history, to that point, ended 18:28 into the extra period when Bob Murdoch passed to Bob Nevin, who then gave the puck to Goring, who crossed the blue line, cut to his left, and beat Cheevers with a shot just inside the left goal post. The series was tied, 3-3. Fans at the Forum that night will long remember the Kings streaming off the bench and carrying Goring off the ice on their shoulders, the first and only time I've ever seen that in a hockey game. On the air, I was screaming, 'We're going back to Boston, we're going back to Boston for Game 7!'

A great sportswriter in Boston named Leigh Montville wrote a column titled "Kings of the Living Dead." He said Game 7 was the game no one in Boston thought would ever be played, and yet every time the Bruins think the Kings are dead, 'the Kings stick their fingers over the side of the coffin each time the lid is about to close. Two weeks ago the Kings were a curiosity in Boston, now it's time to be afraid of the L.A. Kings. Man should always be afraid of things that won't die.' Well, the Kings couldn't stay alive in

Game 7, as Boston's backup goalie Gilles Gilbert won a 3-0 shutout.

The last event ever held in the Boston Garden was on September 28, 1995, a preseason game between the Bruins and the Canadiens. The Garden then sat vacant for two years before it was torn down, and the land now serves as a parking lot for the current home of the Bruins, TD Garden. What can't be demolished, however, are the memories of the great teams and players who once played in the "Gah-den."

MAPLE LEAF GARDENS

The hockey arena, considered by many in Canada to be the "Shrine" of hockey, stood on the corner of Carleton and Church streets in Toronto, Ontario. The home of the Toronto Maple

Leafs was also known as the "Carleton Street Cashbox" because the Leafs sold out every home game from 1946 to 1999.

The popularity of Maple Leaf Gardens was probably due to the fact that from 1938 to 1970, only two Canadian teams were in the NHL. The mystique of the Gardens was enhanced every Saturday night when most of Canada gathered around the radio to listen to "Hockey Night in Canada" and hear the "original" voice of hockey, Foster Hewitt, sign on his broadcast with 'Hello Canada and hockey fans in the United States and Newfoundland.' Newfoundland was an independent dominion before joining Canada in 1949.

Maple Leaf Gardens was built in 1931 at the cost of $1.5 million Canadian dollars. It was built in an unparalleled five months and two weeks. The first game was on November 12, 1931, with the Leafs losing to Chicago, 2-1. The Leafs went on that season to win their first Stanley Cup. Prior to that season, the Toronto team was known as the "St. Patricks" and prior to that, the "Arenas."

I was never that fond of Maple Leaf Gardens. My impression was that since they sold out every game, they didn't care much about the media or public relations. The first Kings game I ever televised was on KTLA from Maple Leaf Gardens. Hewitt — who broadcast Leafs games for some 52 years—was in the booth next to me, and sometimes during a lull in the action I would lean over to see if I could hear what he was saying.

I even had the opportunity to interview the Hall of Fame legend between periods.

I must say, however, that if I hadn't known the Toronto franchise had been around since 1917, I would have thought they had been in existence for about two weeks. The game notes given to the media before each game were laughable. There was little or no information about the players but they contained such notes as, "Happy Birthday to Joe, the usher in section 102," or the best of all-time, "The Leafs welcome 300 Inuit priests to the game tonight. They are in town to translate the Bible into Inuit" (I actually used that note on our Kings telecast).

Our broadcast location started out in the famous "gondola" where Hewitt broadcast from, and it was a decent view of the game. Then it switched to the other side of the arena in the main press box where we were separated from writers and other broadcasters by just a small temporary partition, then back to the gondola where the visitors were given a tiny space with barely enough room for three people.

Two distinct occurrences stand out in my memory of Maple Leaf Gardens, one negative and the other positive. The negative took place March 2, 1981. It was the night Charlie Simmer, the Kings' leading goal scorer at the time with 56 goals in 65 games, suffered a spiral fracture of his right leg. Always with a sense of humor, Charlie said, 'If you're going to break your leg, do it on Saturday night on Hockey Night in Canada so everyone can see it. Don't do it on a Thursday night in Pittsburgh.'

The positive was the Western Conference Final playoff series in 1993 between the Kings and Maple Leafs. I think that was the most intense, classic series I have ever seen.

Both team captains, Wayne Gretzky of the Kings and Wendell Clark of the Leafs, stood up to lead their teams. Marty McSorley set the physical tone in Game 1 in Toronto, with a vicious check on Doug Gilmour, and then Clark stepped in to fight McSorley. Even the coaches got involved when the Leafs' Pat Burns tried to get to the Kings bench and told Kings Head Coach Barry Melrose, who had shoulder length hair, to get a haircut. Melrose then puffed out his cheeks, indicating that Burns was fat and said he thought Burns was just trying to go get another hot dog. As the series progressed, the Leafs won Game 5 in the Gardens to take a 3-2 lead in the series. The Kings had to win Game 6 at home or be eliminated. Clark had a hat trick and scored his third goal with only 1:21 left in regulation to send the game to overtime. Gretzky then won the game for the Kings 1:41 into overtime and we were set for Game 7 in Maple Leaf Gardens with the winner going to the Stanley Cup Final.

Game 7 was on May 29, 1993 and was one of the greatest games I've ever had the pleasure of calling. Gretzky had a hat trick, and with a little over a minute left the Kings led 5-3. But with 1:07 remaining, Dave Ellett scored for Toronto and the Kings' lead was cut to only one goal. The final minute was so hectic, and as the Leafs were buzzing around the Kings' goal, I was sweating, shaking, and telling myself to settle down. With five seconds left, the Kings cleared the puck to center ice and on our telecast I shouted, 'The Kings are four wins away from the Stanley Cup.'

Jim Fox and I broadcast that series from the top of the gondola, over a hundred feet above the ice. That famous Hewitt gondola was dismantled and dumped into an incinerator in August, 1979 to make room for private boxes.

Maple Leaf Gardens was known for several innovations. It was the first arena to have plexi-glass in the end zones in the 1946-47 season. On November 8, 1963, it was the first arena in the NHL to have separate penalty boxes. Former Kings Head Coach Bob Pulford told me that happened because until then both players went into the same penalty box. The visitor would go in first, followed by the home team player. One night in the Gardens, Pulford, who played for Toronto, and Terry Harper, who played for Montreal and later was a Kings captain under Pulford, both received penalties. Harper went in the box first, and while he was seated there Pulford hauled off and punched him. They rolled around fighting in the box, and police were called. It was then decided it would be best to have separate penalty boxes.

The final game in Maple Leaf Gardens was on February 13, 1999, when the Leafs lost to the Chicago Blackhawks, 6-2. The Gardens still stands, but it was converted into a Loblaws grocery store and an athletic center for Ryerson University. The renovation was completed in the summer of 2012, and the building is the new home of the Ryerson Rams hockey team. Thus, it is the only arena of the so-called "Original Six" teams to be used for hockey.

MONTREAL FORUM

One of the most famous hockey arenas, and the one housing the most Stanley Cup Championships, was the Montreal Forum in Quebec, Canada. Built in 1924 at the corner of Atwater and St. Catherine Street, it was the home of the Montreal Canadiens from 1926 to 1996. It cost $1.5 million to build, and in today's money that would be $20 million. The final NHL game in the Forum was on March 11, 1996, as the Canadiens beat the Dallas Stars 4-1. In between the first and last games in the building, the teams that played there won 26 Stanley Cup Championships, two by the Montreal Maroons and 24 by the Canadiens.

My memories of broadcasting Kings games in the Montreal Forum:

- The sense of history as you walked into the main lobby. Photos of all the great Canadiens hanging on the walls, Hall of Famers such as Jean Beliveau, Rocket Richard, Toe Blake, coach Dick Irvin, "Boom Boom" Geoffrion, Doug Harvey and others.

- The 24 Stanley Cup banners hanging from the rafters, more than any other building in the NHL.

- The steepness of the seats. In the eighth row of the lower red seats, you were already above the glass.

- Like many old arenas, there was not a decent press box for radio and TV, since the building was built before television existed. However, we did have a magnificent view of the game, with a steep angle and close to the ice. We also did not have a television studio for pre- and post-game shows like we have today. In fact, our "studio" was in the garage area of the arena with fumes from automobiles and the zamboni.

- We would do between-period interviews on the ice. Rich Marotta was my partner in the mid-70s, and one night he went down to the ice surface to interview Bob Gainey of Montreal. We discovered that Rich's microphone would not work, so they told me to go on camera and fill the time. The score was only 1-0 so there wasn't a lot to talk about, and I was by myself with no one to interview. I filled for about five minutes and felt I was doing a wonderful job, when finally Rich's mic was working and I threw down to him. The phone rang in our booth and it was someone from Los Angeles who told me Kings owner Jack Kent Cooke had called. I thought he called to congratulate me on the job I did filling the time, but he said to tell me to "quit hogging the mic and let Rich talk once in a while."

- The spine-tingling rendition of "O Canada" by Roget Doucet, who sang the national anthems in the Forum in the '70s.

- Watching and describing thrilling rushes up the ice by Guy LaFleur, Yvan Cournoyer and Steve Shutt.

- The Kings Stanley Cup Final series vs. Montreal in 1993, and Marty McSorley's infamous illegal stick in Game 2. Montreal won Game 5 by a score of 4-1 to win their 24th and last Stanley Cup to this date.

Today a portion of the old Forum still stands, and inside it has been converted to restaurants and movie theatres, but no amount of renovations can erase the great memories of one of the greatest shrines of hockey.

THE FABULOUS FORUM

In my opinion, the most distinctive and beautiful Forum was the home of the Los Angeles Kings from 1967 to 1999. It was built for the sum of $16 million and that included the land, and it was designed in a circular "Roman Forum" design that was so distinctive that when you saw a photo of it you knew immediately that it was the Forum in Inglewood, California. Owner Jack Kent Cooke demanded that we call it the "Fabulous Forum." The name changed in December of 1988 when then owner Dr. Jerry Buss sold the naming rights to Great Western Savings and Loan. That was the first naming rights deal in American sports at that time, and the building became known as "The Great Western Forum."

I broadcast Kings' games in that building from 1973 to 1999, before the Kings moved to STAPLES Center. I have so many memories from that building that I could not list them all in this space. Some of them include:

- The availability to visit with fans in what was a somewhat intimate setting compared to the huge arenas of today.

- The lack of a "formal" press box. Apparently the architect, who also designed the current Madison Square Garden in New York, forgot there "might" be media coverage in the two largest markets in the U.S.

- Therefore, the "press box" took up several rows of seats in the front rows of the colonnade at center ice. It had a decent view of the game, but there were times that fans in the lower bowl would stand and block our view and that of the TV cameras. The biggest problem I had was with the "cotton candy man" when he had a full pallet and would stop in front of me. I had to look around the cotton candy to describe the play.

- The accessibility fans had to the broadcast location. One night while I was doing the play-by-play, I felt a tap on my shoulder and a Kings fan said, 'Hey, Bob, I want to ask you a question.' Needless to say I was a little busy at the time.

- The 1981 All-Star Game that featured the Kings' Triple Crown line of Marcel Dionne, Dave Taylor and Charlie Simmer, all introduced together to the crowd. Kings goalie Mario Lessard was also on that All-Star team.

- The 1993 Stanley Cup Final, when the Kings met the Montreal Canadiens. Before the Kings' first home game in that series, I saw fans toasting each other with champagne in their seats, finally seeing something they had never seen before in the Forum.

- The "Miracle on Manchester" playoff game on April 10, 1982, against the powerful Edmonton Oilers. The underdog Kings trailed 5-0 at the end of two periods but rallied with five goals in the third period, the tying goal by Steve Bozek with five seconds left. In overtime, the Kings won the game on a blistering shot by Daryl Evans for a 6-5 win, and the Kings subsequently went on to win the series.

- Wayne Gretzky's first regular season game in a Kings uniform (October 6, 1988). He scored on his first shot in an 8-2 win over Detroit.

- Of course, there were so many others, but time and space here doesn't permit.

The final game in The Great Western Forum was on April 18, 1999. Thousands of Kings fans still have extremely fond memories of the "Fabulous Forum."

THE SPECTRUM, PHILADELPHIA

Not many NHL players on opposing teams enjoyed playing in the Spectrum, which was one of the most intimidating venues in the NHL. It was located on Broad Street in the South Philadelphia Sports Complex and was the home of the Philadelphia Flyers, known in the early 1970s as the "Broad Street Bullies," because of their belligerent and physical style of play. When visiting players, for whatever reason, couldn't play in a game there, they were accused of having the "Philadelphia Flu," a fictitious illness.

The Spectrum opened in the fall of 1967 after taking only 11 months to build at a cost of $12 million, or in 2012 dollars, $83.6 million. It was Philadelphia's first modern indoor sports arena, and opening night concession prices featured a hot dog for 35 cents, a roast beef sandwich for 75 cents, an eight-ounce soft drink for 15 cents, and a 12-ounce soft drink for 25 cents. A regular beer cost 10 cents and a premium beer 40 cents.

The Flyers' first-ever home game in the Spectrum featured a 1-0 victory over the Pittsburgh Penguins. The LA Kings' first-ever game in the arena was on November 26, 1967, a 7-2 loss to the Flyers, with Terry Gray and Real Lemieux scoring the Kings' goals. Wayne Rutledge played 31 minutes in goal and allowed five goals, and Terry Sawchuck played 29 minutes and allowed the final two goals. My first Kings broadcast in the Spectrum was on November 8, 1973, a 3-2 Kings victory. The Kings scored in each period on goals by Mike Corrigan, Butch Goring and Whitey Widing. Gary Edwards stopped 33 of 35 Flyers shots. The Kings did not win a lot of games in the Spectrum, but one memorable victory took place on opening night, October 10, 1974. The Flyers had become the first of the 1967 expansion teams to win the Stanley Cup the previous season. They planned a huge celebration for that opening night, complete with the Stanley Cup, raising the championship banner, and their "good luck" charm, famous singer Kate Smith there in person to sing "God Bless America." The Kings spoiled the festivities, beating the Flyers, 5-3, on goals by Mike Corrigan, Bob Murdoch, Dan Maloney, and two by Tommy Williams. Gary Edwards was the winning Kings goalie, facing 37 Flyers shots.

There were several wild occurrences at the Spectrum in games between the Kings and Flyers. When the press box and broadcast location was in the lower bowl, fans would pass by writers and broadcasters on the way to their seats. Every time the Kings played there, an elderly gentleman would stop in front of me with a puppet dressed in a Flyers uniform and say in his German accent, 'Dis is vat Schultz vill do to de Kings tonight,' and he would pull a string and the Flyers puppet would throw punches at another puppet dressed in a Kings uniform. That is exactly what happened on the night of March 11, 1979. In the first period of that game, 372 penalty minutes were handed out, and 10 players were ejected from the game. Kings players ejected were: Randy Holt, Mark Heaslip, Steve Jensen, Dave Taylor and Bert Wilson. My biggest memory of that brawl was of the Flyers' Ken "The Rat" Linseman skating around players who were paired off fighting. He was trying to trip Kings' players with his stick. He had an appropriate nickname. At the time, that game set NHL records in nine penalty categories. Holt of the Kings still has the NHL individual record for most penalties in one period (9); most penalty minutes in one period (67); and most penalty minutes in one game (67). The Flyers won the game, 6-3, giving them a record of 15-0-4 in the last 19 games vs. the Kings.

Weather has been a factor in Spectrum history. On March 1, 1968, wind blew part of the covering off the roof, forcing the closure of the building for one month. The Flyers hurriedly moved their next "home game" to Madison Square Garden in New York, then played a "home game" in Toronto's Maple Leaf Gardens, and finished the remainder of their "home schedule" in the Coliseum in Quebec City, home of their top minor league team. They were able to return to the Spectrum for their first playoff game that season against the St. Louis Blues on April 4, 1968.

Mother Nature showed her wrath again on March 13, 1993, when the Kings played at the Spectrum. During the first period, a storm dubbed "The Storm of the Century," with 50 mph winds and 12 inches of snow, hit the East Coast. The winds shattered a sizeable pane of glass on the concourse, and the building was deemed unsafe. The game was suspended at the end of the period, with the score tied 1-1. The game was postponed until April 1 and played from the start, with the Kings winning 3-1 on goals by Luc Robitaille, Rob Blake, and Darryl Sydor.

Weather and poor scheduling also played a part in a Kings game at the Spectrum on January 7, 1979. The night before, the Kings played in Pittsburgh, and the next day they flew to Philadelphia. Due to ice and snow, the Kings' plane couldn't land in Philly and was diverted to Kennedy airport in New York, all of this on a game day. The Kings scrambled to charter a bus to Philadelphia and went right to the arena, arriving at 5:20 PM for a 7 PM game. We were live on television at 7 PM for the start of the game, when it was announced the game wouldn't start until 7:30 PM The ice wasn't ready, due to a gymnastics event at the arena earlier in the day, so we had an impromptu 30 minutes to fill.

My partner at the time, Pete Weber, and I filled the half hour with comments and interviews. At one point while I was "on camera," I noticed something in my peripheral vision, but I didn't look away. When we went to a commercial break, Pete said to me, 'Did you see the size of that rat running along the TV cable?' Luckily I hadn't. The late arrival and the delay in starting the game didn't help the Kings, as they lost 3-0, with Flyers goalie Bernie Parent getting his 55th career shutout.

Kings Head Coach Bob Pulford got into trouble at the Spectrum on October 10, 1976. During another fight-filled game, a bench-clearing brawl broke out in the first period.

During the fight, an incensed Pulford grabbed the jersey of linesman John Brown and shook him. Realizing he was in trouble, Pulford started smoothing out Brown's shirt. Pulford was ejected and fined the "exorbitant" amount of $350. The Kings had no assistant coaches in those days, so General Manger Jake Milford coached the remainder of the game, which was won by the Flyers, 1-0.

In later years, the broadcast location was moved to the third level of the building, and the only bathroom facilities were on the first floor, open to the public, and no elevator. On November 3, 1985, with eight minutes left in the game, I was in trouble, as nature was calling and I knew I couldn't wait until the end of the game, nor could I make it downstairs to the public bathroom. So, just as many announcers have done so during their careers, I was forced to use empty soft drink cups to rescue me.

The Flyers won back to back Stanley Cups in 1974 and 1975, and on January 11, 1976, during the height of the Cold War, they became the first NHL team to defeat the vaunted Central Red Army team of the Soviet Union by a score of 4-1 in Philadelphia.

The Flyers truly enjoyed a "home ice" advantage in the Spectrum, as they still hold the NHL record for the longest undefeated streak in one season, 35 games in 1979-80 with 25 wins and 10 ties. They achieved many of those wins in front of the boisterous home crowd.

The Flyers played their final game in the Spectrum in Game 5 of the 1996 Eastern Conference Semifinals, losing to the Florida Panthers in overtime. The Flyers subsequently moved into their new home – then called the Wells Fargo Center – for the 1996-97 season.

The Flyers' minor league team, the Phantoms, then played at the Spectrum until the building was demolished, starting in November of 2010. A "wrecking ball ceremony" was held with Flyers greats, including Hall of Famers Bobby Clarke and Bernie Parent, in attendance. The demolition was completed in May of 2011 without the use of explosives.

I'm sure no opposing player shed a tear over the demolition.

PITTSBURGH CIVIC ARENA, "THE IGLOO"

The most unique building in the National Hockey League was originally known as the Pittsburgh Civic Arena but was more commonly known by its more popular name "The Igloo," Home of the Pittsburgh Penguins from 1967 to 2010. The name "Igloo" came from the construction of the dome roof supported by a 260-foot-long cantilevered arm on the exterior of the building. It was the first retractable roof built for a major sports venue worldwide.

The building was constructed in 1961 for use by the Pittsburgh Civic Light Opera at a cost of $22 million dollars, which would equal 171 million in 2012 dollars. The hydraulic jacks never functioned properly, so the roof was permanently kept closed after 1994.

The Pittsburgh Hornets of the American Hockey League played in the arena from 1961 to 1967, when the Penguins became part of the NHL expansion. The Penguins' first game was played on October 11, 1967, a 2-1 loss to the Montreal Canadiens. It was the first game played between an expansion team and a member of the "Original Six". On October 21 of that year, the Penguins became the first expansion team to defeat an "original" NHL franchise, as they beat the Chicago Blackhawks 4-2.

The Los Angeles Kings played their first game at the Igloo on October 28, 1967 and beat the Penguins 5-3. That Kings roster featured players such as Eddie "The Jet" Joyal, "Cowboy" Bill Flett, and goaltender Terry Sawchuck. My first broadcast in the building was on January 16, 1974, which the Kings won 2-0.

One of my most fond memories of games in "The Igloo" was of listening to their popular organist Vince Lascheid. In the early years of the arena, the organ was located just to my left in the press box, so I had a full view of Vince as he played. He would play songs designed to get under the skin of opposing teams. In our games, when the Kings would come from their dressing room, Vince would be playing the song, "Send in the Clowns." I would always smile and give Vince a thumbs up sign for his impeccable timing. Lascheid was the Penguins' organist from 1970 to 2003 in the era when the organ was the instrument of choice for music at all hockey games, and in my opinion was so much better than the loud canned music of today. Vince Lascheid is in the Penguins Hall of Fame and passed away in 2009 at age 85.

We always had fun in Pittsburgh, and I remember one night, December 14, 1993 after the Kings beat the Penguins 4-2, a group of us went to a karaoke bar. A group of Penguin fans recognized some of us and asked, "Are you guys with the Kings?" When we said yes, they began to boo. I told them, "I am going to get up and sing a song in honor of the Penguins defense."

Then they started to cheer and asked, "What are you going to sing?" I said I was going to sing "Blue Bayou".

The greatest player I ever saw play at the Igloo was Mario Lemieux, who could control a game like no other player. He was almost unstoppable on the power play. My good friend, the late coach Bob Johnson, whom I met while I was broadcasting University of Wisconsin hockey, led the Penguins to a Stanley Cup championship in 1991. His favorite phrase was, "It's a Great Day for Hockey." After he passed away, that phrase was on the ice at the Igloo, and it always had special meaning for me each time I worked in the building.

In later years, the arena became known as Mellon Arena, named for Mellon Financial, which had naming rights. The Penguins played their final game at Mellon Arena on May 12, 2010 and lost to Montreal 5-2, which eliminated them from the Stanley Cup Playoffs in Game Seven of the Eastern Conference Semifinals.

The Penguins now play in their sparkling new home, the Consol Energy Center, which is located right across the street from the old arena. The Civic Arena, Mellon Arena, or The Igloo, whichever name you preferred, was demolished between September 2011 and March 31, 2012.

"THE AUD," BUFFALO, NEW YORK

The Buffalo Memorial Auditorium was simply referred to as "The Aud" by those fans living in Buffalo. The building opened on October 14, 1940. It was built for $2.7 million, which in 2012 money would be $45.1 million. It was the home of the Buffalo Bisons of the American Hockey League from 1940 -1970, the Buffalo Bisons of the National Basketball League in 1946, the Buffalo Sabres of the NHL from 1970-1996, and the Buffalo Braves of the NBA from 1970-1978.

The Buffalo Sabres played their first game in The Aud on October 15, 1970, and their final game there at the end of the 1995-96 season, a 4-1 victory over the Hartford Whalers.

Like most arenas of the time, seating was steep and provided an outstanding, close-up view of the action. Talk about a crowd "raising the roof"— in 1971, the roof was actually raised 24 feet, making room for a new upper "orange" level," and increasingthe capacity to 15,858 for hockey. The Aud was located in downtown Buffalo, at one end of what was once the Erie Canal. It became the center of entertainment in Buffalo and was also the last of the NHL arenas in which the ice surface was not the regulation size of 200 by 85 feet.

The Aud was 196 by 85 feet, Boston Garden was 191 by 83 feet, Chicago Stadium was 188 by 85 feet, and the Detroit Olympia was 200 by 83 feet.

Hockey fans were treated to a lot of thrilling games in The Aud, including one on February 24, 1982, when Wayne Gretzky of the visiting Edmonton Oilers scored a "natural" hat trick in the final seven minutes to defeat the Sabres, 6-3. The first goal of that hat trick was Gretzky's 77th of the season, breaking the record of 76 held by Phil Esposito. I did not see that game, but here are some of the things I do remember about working in The Aud:

- The most exciting line in hockey at the time, the "French Connection Line" of Gilbert Perreault, Rene Robert and Rick Martin. Until the L.A. Kings Triple Crown Line came along in the early 80s, the French Connection Line could bring you right out of your seat. I always said when Perreault stick-handled up the ice it was like listening to someone using a typewriter as he deftly handled the stick and puck.

- The television location was in an area called "The Bucket." It was a small platform hanging off the ledge of the upper deck. It had a great view of the game, but you had to walk down through the crowd, climb over the railing and down a short ladder to get to your spot. The main press box was located at the top of that section.

- In those years, we did Kings hockey on a simulcast, meaning radio and TV at the same time. One night, the radio lines were mistakenly put in a booth in the main press box, but my partner, Nick Nickson, and I were located in "The Bucket." Since during the intermissions we did separate radio and TV audio, this posed a problem and we didn't have time to change it. Therefore, at the end of each period, Nick would go downstairs to do a TV interview, and I would go up to the radio booth. When Nick finished the interview, he would come back to "The Bucket," and I would lean over the press box railing to cue him for the television portion and I would do radio. At the end of that segment, during a commercial, I would go back down to "The Bucket" for the next period, and at the next intermission we'd do it all over again.

- Buffalo has a reputation for snow...a lot of snow, and sudden snowstorms. On January 10, 1982, the area was hit by a sudden blizzard. Over 15,000 tickets had been sold for the Kings-Sabres game, but only 2,079 brave souls made it to The Aud. In fact, on the bridge behind the auditorium, people had to abandon their cars and be led off the bridge holding on to ropes. During the game, the Sabres announced that fans that were stranded and couldn't get home could spend the night in The Aud or in the Sabres offices. The next morning, a photo in the

Buffalo newspaper showed a fan sleeping in the penalty box.

- After that "blizzard" game, all Kings personnel were told to go to the back door of the arena where a four-wheel drive vehicle would take them back to the hotel, which was only about a quarter of a mile away. When I got to the back door, about 50 people were ahead of me, the vehicle was able to take only three people at a time, and it was taking about 45 minutes for the round trip. I decided to walk. I used my broadcast headset as earmuffs and started in the general direction of the hotel because you couldn't see anything in the complete "white out." During my walk I thought, 'I'm not going to make it.' When I finally got to my room, I noticed a quarter-size area of skin on my face that looked like the beginning of frost-bite. By the way, the Kings lost that game, 6-4.

The Aud, and Buffalo, were not favorite spots on the road for most NHL teams. The Aud closed in 1996 and demolition was started in January of 2009, and by early July of that year The Aud, which was at one time the showplace of Buffalo and which held so many memories for Sabres fans, was completely gone.

KEMPER ARENA

The Kansas City Scouts of the National Hockey League played in Kemper Arena in Kansas City, Missouri, for two seasons – 1974-75 and 1975-76 – before moving to Denver. They were not very successful, to say the least, winning only 27 games, losing 110 and tying 23 in those two seasons.

Kemper Arena was built in 18 months in 1973-74 at a cost of $22 million. It stood on the site of the former Kansas City

Stockyards, just west of downtown. Capacity for hockey was 17,647.

The Los Angeles Kings played a total of four games in Kemper, winning three and losing one. One Kings win especially stands out in my memory.

The date was March 30, 1976, and the Scouts were in the midst of another terrible season in which they wound up losing 56 games, and winning only 12. However, on this night the Scouts jumped out to a 3-0 lead over Los Angeles on goals by former Kings player Randy Rota, and Denis Dupere and Jim McElmury in the first 8:21 of the game against Kings goalie Rogie Vachon. The Kings then started a comeback on goals by Tommy Williams and Larry Brown. After K.C. took a 6-5 lead at the end of the second period, the Kings next scored two consecutive goals by Mike Corrigan and Bob Murdoch to take a 7-6 lead. This upset the Scouts fans that proceeded to litter the ice with game programs, beer and soft drinks.

Our broadcast location in Kemper was in one of the suites just at the top of the lower bowl with the fans seated down in front of us. At the time I said on our radio broadcast, 'This shows the mentality of these fans, stupidly littering the ice with debris.' The fans could hear our comments, and I heard one fan say in a loud, gruff voice, 'Did you hear what he said about us?' I looked down and this angry man, about 6'5", stood up and came toward our booth. He didn't go in to the aisle, instead he just started stepping over the backs of seats to get to us. He leaned on the short glass in front of me and stared at me from about a foot in front of my face. I wasn't sure what he was going to do, perhaps throw a soft drink in my face or something worse. My partner, Dan Avey, was swinging his handheld microphone as if he was ready to use it to hit the fan. Dan then told a little usherette to go get security. She left and never returned, nor did security. I had to look around the fan to do the play-by-play, and I was determined not to let him distract me.

When Williams scored his third goal of the game to give the Kings the lead, I really poured it on, just to upset the fan even more. By this time he was spitting mad and in his frustration he tore up his ticket stubs, threw them at me and said, 'I'll see you later.' You could come into our booth from the concourse so I spent the rest of the game alternating between calling the play-by-play and looking over my shoulder, but my "friend" never showed up. The Kings won the game 8-6 in their final appearance in Kemper Arena.

The new Sprint Center in Kansas City opened in 2007, managed by the Kings owners, Anschutz Entertainment Group. Kemper Arena still stands and in 2013 will be the home of the Kansas City Renegades of the Champions Professional Indoor Football League.

The Scouts played only two seasons in Kansas City before moving to Denver to become the Colorado Rockies of the NHL. After six seasons in Denver, the franchise moved to New Jersey and became the very successful New Jersey Devils.

McNICHOLS ARENA

In 1976, the Kansas City Scouts moved to Denver, Colorado, and became the Colorado Rockies of the NHL. The Rockies played in McNichols Arena, completed in 1975 at a cost of $16 million and which seated 16,061 for hockey.

The L.A. Kings' first game in McNichols Arena was on November 28, 1976, and the game ended in a 6-6 tie in front of only 5,697 fans. Tommy Williams and Lorne Stamler each scored two goals for the Kings, who built a 6-3 lead. Denis Dupere had two of three unanswered goals for the Rockies to force the tie.

The radio-TV and press facilities at McNichols were not ideal, to say the least. A makeshift press box was set up for writers at one end of the arena behind the goal. It was a terrible view of the play at the opposite end over 200 feet away. The television booth was located at center ice, but it also had its flaws. Once we were seated, the only way for my partner, Nick Nickson, to leave the booth for an interview was to crawl through an open window frame out into the crowd. He was fortunate that there was no glass in the frame.

During the intermission, I would go on camera to give out of town scores and comment on what went on in the period. To go on camera, either at the open of the telecast or between periods, we had to stand on folding chairs with the danger of collapsing. To prevent falling, I would hold on with one hand to a railing in front of us. It was not viewable on camera, so I don't think viewers ever knew how precarious the situation was. Of course, they would have if we suddenly fell out of camera view, which fortunately never happened.

The Rockies played six seasons in Denver and made the play-offs one time, losing in the first round. The Rockies then moved to New Jersey to become the Devils, starting with the 1982-83 season. The NHL was absent in Denver from 1982 until 1995, when the Quebec Nordiques moved to Denver to become the Colorado Avalanche.

In their first season in Denver, 1995-96, the Avalanche won the Stanley Cup. Former L.A. King and U.S. Hockey Hall of Fame member Eddie Olczyk and I broadcast a playoff game for NHL Radio between the Avalanche and the Detroit Red Wings that season. When the Nordiques arrived in Denver at the start of the season, very few people were familiar with the players, but by playoff time almost everyone in Denver was wearing an Avalanche jersey with a player's name on the back. I went into the gift shop at the hotel in which I was staying, and an elderly woman working there asked me in her faltering voice, 'Do you think the Avalanche can win the Stanley Cup?' I answered, 'Oh, I hope so, you've been waiting so long, what is it now, six months?'

During the pre-game warm-up for that playoff game, all the lights went out on our side of the arena but not over the ice or the opposite stands. Olczyk and I started our broadcast on the telephone, passing it back and forth to make comments. That lasted through two periods before the lights returned on our side of the arena.

McNichols Arena was demolished on January 24, 2000, after the Avalanche moved into the new Pepsi Center in 1999. I don't believe any broadcasters were sorry to see McNichols fade into history.

ALAMEDA COUNTY COLISEUM ARENA, OAKLAND

The California Seals, later to become the Oakland Seals and then the California Golden Seals, entered the National Hockey League along with the Los Angeles Kings and four other teams in the expansion of 1967. They played their games in the Oakland-Alameda County Coliseum Arena, which was located in the Coliseum industrial area.

It is a circular building built with a steel frame and glass surrounding the entire structure.

The building was built in 1966 at a cost of $25 million, which would be $179 million in 2012 dollars. It was elevated so that when you entered the building you were about 50 rows up looking down at the ice surface. The building still stands, and the interior was completely rebuilt in 1996-97 at a cost of $121 million, but the external walls, roof, and foundation remained intact and it is now known as Oracle Arena.

The Kings' first game in the arena was on October 18, 1967, and it ended in a 2-2 tie. What I remember most about playing the Seals is that many of our games would be on a Sunday afternoon around 2 p.m. The Kings would usually have a home game the night before, and Western Airlines would hold their midnight flight until the Kings could get to LAX for the short flight to Oakland. The Kings would head right back home after the Sunday game and be back in L.A. by 7 p.m., with a road trip out of the way. Some of you may remember a group that called themselves, "The White Hats," and I believe most of them were Western Airlines employees. They would sit at one end of the Forum, then march around the inner concourse, leading cheers for the Kings while wearing a variety of white hats. Some of them would always join us on the flight to Oakland.

Something else that stood out in Oakland was the Seals' mascot called "Crazy George." He looked a little crazy and would roam the arena with a small drum that he would incessantly pound to inspire the crowd and intimidate the opposing players. Many times he would almost hang over the glass, and players would be startled if they weren't aware that he was right over their shoulder.

Hockey was a tough sell in the Bay Area in those years, and in their first season the Seals won only 15 of 74 games and finished last in the Western Division. They were the lowest scoring team in the NHL with only 153 goals, and the crowds were usually small.

In fact, only 3,419 fans showed up for the Kings' first game in the arena. In 1969, the Kings and Seals met in the opening round of the playoffs, which the Kings won four games to three. That was the only time the teams met each other in the playoffs. My first broadcast in the arena was on January 2, 1974, when the Seals beat the Kings 5-2 in front of a paltry crowd of 2,860.

The Seals had several owners, the most famous of whom was Charles O. Finley, the flamboyant owner of baseball's Oakland Athletics. One of his marketing gimmicks was to change the team's colors to Kelly Green and California Gold and have the team wear white skates, which the players hated. At the end of the 1970 season, the Seals traded their number-one pick in the first round of the 1971 draft to Montreal. Due to the Seals finishing last in the NHL in 1970-71, Montreal had the number-one pick and took future Hall of Famer, Guy LaFleur, so the deal was one of the most lopsided in NHL history.

After being frustrated by several losing seasons, Finley tried to sell the team but had no takers, so the NHL took over the team in February 1974, purchasing it from Finley for $6.5 million dollars. In July of 1976, the League approved a relocation of the team to Cleveland, where they became the Barons; thus the Kings had lost their closest opponent geographically. Attendance was worse in Cleveland than it had been in Oakland, and after two years of losses the Barons merged with the Minnesota North Stars.

The last Seals player to be active in any league was former Kings player Charlie Simmer, who played with the San Diego Gulls of the International Hockey League until 1992.

The arena in Oakland still stands and is the current home of the Golden State Warriors of the NBA.

3

FIRST PERIOD

THE OWNERS

JACK KENT COOKE

Jack Kent Cooke, the former owner of the Los Angeles Kings, Lakers, and the Forum was small in physical stature but was a giant in the sports and business world. By the time he passed away on April 6, 1997 at age 84, he had accumulated close to a billion dollars. He didn't inherit this money; he started out selling soap to hotels, and then selling encyclopedia sets door to door in his native Canada.

The story goes that one Sunday evening, Cooke and his new wife found themselves in a little town in Saskatchewan with no money to buy dinner that night. Cooke found the home of a high school principal and convinced him to give him a five-dollar deposit on a set of encyclopedias. He then had enough money for food.

He stood only about 5-foot-9, was always impeccably dressed, in a dark suit or blazer always with a silk handerkerchief in the breast pocket. He had a booming stentorian voice. He peered at you through slits in his eyelids, but he could look right through you—especially if he was upset over something you had said or done.

One could use any number of adjectives to describe his personality: tyrannical, overbearing, shrewd, impressive, intelligent, and dynamic. He was the epitome of a "hands-on" owner, one who was domineering and controlled every facet of his empire, which included not only the Kings, Lakers, and Forum, but also in later years the Chrysler Building in New York City, Tele-Prompter, and the Washington Redskins of the National Football League. He possessed a wonderful command of the English language and never let anyone forget it, and at times he could be quite condescending. At one time he owned one of the largest radio stations in Toronto, CKEY. In those days, due to the "blue laws" no stores were open on Sundays. Cooke had one man who had worked for some 20 years at the radio station. One day this employee asked Mr. Cooke if he could have Sundays off, feeling that after 20 years he deserved weekends to himself. Mr. Cooke replied, "What would you do in Toronto with Sundays off? Even I wouldn't know what to do if I didn't have my yacht."

I always admired the fact that he was a self-made multimillionaire, had an estimated $900 million when he passed away, but he left a lot to be desired in the manner in which he treated employees. Because of that attitude he lost a lot of good and talented people who simply said they had had enough and quit their jobs.

Employees lived and worked in fear of raising Mr. Cooke's ire. So much so that we always had a lookout who each morning would watch for Mr. Cooke's Bentley to pull into the Forum parking lot. The sentry would then, in Paul Revere fashion, come down the hallway informing us "Mr. Cooke is coming, Mr. Cooke is coming."

Upon hearing that announcement secretaries would pretend to be on the phone, and office doors would quickly shut so that no one would have to see or talk to him. If Cooke saw you, he would usually greet you in a friendly manner, "Good morning, Bob," but then by the time he arrived in his office he would think of something he was upset with you about and summon you to his office. The summons would come in the form of an announcement on the Forum public address system and would boom throughout the building, "BOB MILLER, REPORT TO MR. COOKE'S OFFICE." Everyone then knew you were in trouble and would actually mock you and laugh at you as you headed for Cooke's office, much like a grade school pupil summoned to the principal's office for a scolding.

THE ANNOUNCEMENT

Late afternoon on Friday, June 13, 1975, those of us in the Kings' hockey office were told to report to the office of owner Jack Kent Cooke—general manager Jake Milford, public relations director Mike Hope, my broadcast partner, Dan Avey, and me. When we arrived, we were surprised to see members of the L.A. Lakers staff already seated. Included were Lakers GM Pete Newell, coach Bill Sharman, announcer Chick Hearn, and Forum publicity director Dick White. I was curious to know why, if this was a hockey announcement, were all the basketball folks there; and if it pertained to basketball, why were we there?

At this time, reports arose that the Kings were close to signing Detroit Red Wing star Marcel Dionne, and I hoped that was the reason for the meeting.

Cooke, seated at his desk, announced in his booming voice: "I have called all of you here to announce to you that today we have signed ... the greatest basketball player in the world, Kareem Abdul-Jabbar. I was sitting on a sofa to Cooke's right, and I guess my face showed my disappointment at not hearing Dionne's name.

Cooke looked at me and hollered, "What's wrong with you, Bob? Don't you know anything about sports? I just made this tremendous announcement, and you're sitting there like a bump on a log. Chick, did you see his reaction?"

"Yes, Jack," Chick said, "I did." (Chick was the only employee I knew who could call Cooke "Jack" and get away with it.) At this point, I wasn't too happy with Chick.

"Mr. Cooke," I replied, "I thought you were going to say you had signed Marcel Dionne for the Kings."

"That will be for another day," Cooke replied. "We are going to have a press conference Monday morning here at the Forum, and it will be the greatest sports press conference in history. If any of this leaks out before Monday, you are all fired."

I thought, "This is great … we are going to try to sneak into town—without anyone noticing—a seven-foot tall athlete who played basketball for UCLA? It can't be done. "

"The press conference will be held at 10 a.m." Cooke continued. "When should we notify the media?"

He called upon Dick White, who answered, "We should call the media at 9 a.m. Monday morning."

"Nine a.m. Monday morning?" Cooke bewilderedly asked. "Bob, what do you think?"

I knew he wasn't too pleased with Dick White's answer, so I said, "I think Monday morning is too short notice. I think the hockey people should come in here late Sunday night, and when the sports shows are finished, we call the television and radio stations and inform them of the press conference. That way, they will still think it's hockey related and not basketball."

"Right you are," said Cooke. "Dick White, what am I paying you for?"

I may not have been too pleased with Chick, but Dick White was definitely displeased with me. The meeting was becoming very bizarre.

Again, Cooke turned to me and said, "Bob …" and at that point, I was just hoping that he'd leave me alone and ask someone else. "Bob, you are from *Sports Illustrated*, and you're assigned to cover this press conference. When it's over, do you want a sit-down luncheon or a buffet with chicken cacciatore?"

By then, I was getting into the routine. "Mr. Cooke," I said, "I would be so excited about this announcement and so anxious to write my story that I would like a buffet with chicken cacciatore."

"Right again!" Cooke exclaimed.

At that point, I was thinking, "Can I leave now? I've answered two questions right, and it's not going to get any better than this." On that Sunday night, some of us from the Kings office came in and made calls to the television and radio-station sports departments. Some rumors had arisen about this deal on the air. Cooke came in that Monday morning about nine o'clock, and I'd never seen him so excited. He was dressed to the "nines" and could hardly wait to make his monumental announcement.

The Forum floor was empty aside from a stage at the south end, where the home teams enter and exit the floor. On this stage, Cooke had the operations department put two hockey nets and two basketball backboards to further the charade of whether this was a hockey or basketball announcement. Shortly after he arrived, Cooke came to my office and said, "Bob, let's rehearse the news conference."

He gathered several employees, such as Chick Hearn, who would make the announcement; the organist, who was instructed to play the Lakers March at the proper time; and the spotlight operator, who would beam the light on black curtains through which Abdul-Jabbar would enter.

Hearn went to the podium, made a phony announcement to maintain secrecy, and then Cooke cued the organist. Satisfied, he returned to his office. About 15 minutes later, he came back again. "Bob, let's rehearse once more." Again, Hearn went to the podium, the organist climbed to his perch, the spotlight operator was summoned, and we rehearsed—it went off without a hitch.

At 10 a.m., the Forum floor was filled with numerous reporters, television cameras, and microphones. At a table next to the stage and near the podium sat Jack Kent Cooke, Pete Newell, and Bill Sharman. Chick Hearn approached the podium, and, in a voice that sounded as if he were hyperventilating, he made this announcement:

"Ladies and gentlemen, introducing the newest Los Angeles Laker, the most dominant player in the NBA—Kareem Abdul-Jabbar."

With that, the lights dimmed; the organist played; and the spotlight focused on the curtains. No one came out. The music continued and, still, no one appeared.

By this time, some of the reporters began to laugh along with other members of the audience, and I thought, "This is so embarrassing for Cooke that we'll all be fired."

Finally, a pair of black hands parted the curtain, which relieved all of us, feeling, "Abdul-Jabbar must be here." Unfortunately, a uniformed security guard stuck his hat and head through the opening. Now, the laughter increased. A short time later, Kareem appeared, looking confused as he peered into the darkened arena. The reason he was late? The Lakers had hidden him in the locker room, and he went to use the bathroom, where he couldn't hear the announcement.

As it turned out, Cooke was still elated, and no one was fired.

SCOOTING LIKE A DATSUN

One morning in the fall of 1975, Mr. Cooke called my broadcast partner, Dan Avey, and me into his office and told us he wanted to run 14 30-second commercials per period in our Kings broadcasts. At that time, the National Hockey League would not stop the game for radio or TV commercial timeouts. I told Mr. Cooke that I didn't think it would be possible to air that many commercials, because at the time we were running only four per period, and some nights, due to the pace of the game, it was almost impossible to get those on the air.

Our main sponsor at the time was Datsun (now Nissan). "Then you will mention the sponsor's name in a different way," Cooke explained. "For instance you will say, 'There's Marcel Dionne scooting down the ice like a Datsun.' What do you think of that?"

As I listened to him, I remembered the other meetings I had had in Cooke's office with Lakers announcer Chick Hearn. Cooke would come up with some hare-brained ideas, and Chick would respond, "That's a wonderful idea."

As Chick replied, I'd think, "Chick, what are you agreeing to? That's one of the worst ideas I've ever heard."

Then when the meeting was over and we'd walk down the hallway, Chick would complain to me, "That silly bastard. We aren't going to do any of that stuff."

Well, I was determined to stop this idea in its tracks.

"Mr. Cooke," I stated matter-of-factly, "I can't imagine saying that once let alone 80 times a year."

Cooke exploded.

"I'm sick and tired of your attitude!" he thundered. "Do you know how many people want your job, and they're this close [holding his thumb and forefinger a half-inch apart] to getting it."

I smiled at him without saying a word in response, and that set him off even more.

"WIPE THAT SILLY GRIN OFF YOUR FACE AND GET OUT OF MY SIGHT!"

I stood up to leave.

"SIT DOWN!" he roared before I could even take a step toward the door.

I sat.

"Right now it's 11:30 a.m.," he continued. "I want both of you back in here at 2 p.m., and you'd better have some answers for me. NOW, GET OUT!"

Dan and I left his office and walked down the hall. As we did, several secretaries who worked about 100 feet from Cooke's office approached us.

"What did you two guys do?" they asked.

They had heard Cooke yelling at us from that far away.

"Are we fired?" Dan asked with concern.

"Not until 2 p.m.," I replied. "Let's go have some lunch and talk about this."

Over lunch at the Forum Club the conversation turned away from the seriousness of the ultimatum to jokes about the situation.

"You could say, 'The Kings have scored 10 seconds after the start of the game,'" Dan suggested coyly, "and I could say, 'Dat-soon, Dat-soon.'"

That sparked another idea.

"We could give Marcel Dionne No. 280Z," I chuckled, "and Butch Goring could be B-210." (The 280Z and B210 were Datsun model numbers.)

Finally, at 2 p.m. we reappeared in Cooke's office. He stared at me through those beady eyes.

"Well?" he said, commanding an answer.

"Mr. Cooke, we could say, 'The score on the Datsun score-board is Kings 2, Montreal 1,' or 'This is the Datsun-Kings radio network.'"

There was silence as he looked at me.

"My, my," he stated with condescension in his voice, "aren't you a brilliant fellow?"

"Now both of you get out of here."

That was the last we heard about Dionne scooting down the ice like a Datsun.

CONTRACT WHILE WET

The end of my first five-year contract with the Kings was at the end of the 1977-78 season. The Kings that year had finished third in the Norris Division and were getting ready to play the Toronto Maple Leafs in the first round of the playoffs.

On a Sunday afternoon in April my wife and I were swimming and relaxing around the pool at our home, when the phone rang. My wife answered and said to me, "It's for you, it's Mr. Cooke." I said, "Get out of here, he wouldn't be calling me at home."

I got to the phone dripping wet, and Cooke, who never identified himself, he just figured you'd know who it was said, "Bob, I want to talk about your new contract." This took me by surprise, and I was no match for Cooke as far as finance was concerned and especially not while dripping wet on my patio.

He said, "I want you to sign for another five years. Get a paper and pencil and write down these figures. The first year $28,000; the second year, $32,000; the third year, $35,000; the fourth year, 39,000 and the fifth year $43,000, what do you think of that?"

I wanted to make more money but I was scared to mention that to Cooke fearing he would be really upset, but I plunged ahead and said, "Mr. Cooke, I would like to make more money than that." There was a pause and then he said, "Here are the new numbers, write them down." And again he went through the first year, the second year, the third year etc., all with new numbers.

I then felt that I needed more money in years four and five, but I was terrified to make that proposal. However, with all the bravery I could muster I said, "Mr. Cooke, I would like to see the figures for years four and five increased." Holding my breath, my eyes squeezed shut; I then waited for the explosion from the other end of the line. Again, after a pause, Cooke said, "Here are the new numbers, write them down. Year one $35,000; year two $40,000; year three $45,000; year four $51,000 ... then he abruptly paused and said in his booming voice, "My God, we're getting into astronomical numbers."

I thought, "For someone who was signing players for a hell of a lot more, these numbers were not astronomical."

He wanted to know if I was satisfied with the final numbers, and I sensed they were indeed final. A few weeks before this I had received a call from Bob Pulford, then general manager and coach of the Chicago Blackhawks. Pully wanted to know my contract situation and told me not to sign again until I contacted him because he would like me to come to Chicago. When Cooke called I had not yet heard anything from Pulford, so I told thanked Cooke for his offer, but told him I was concentrating on the playoffs and couldn't give him an answer at this time. He asked when I would make a decision and I told him when the playoffs are over. He said, "Fine, and you call me personally with your decision, do not deal with anyone else in the organization."

As bad luck would have it, the Kings were eliminated in two games of a best two-of-three series. However, I thought, I told Cooke when the playoffs ended, that could mean the NHL playoffs not just the Kings playoffs. I kept calling Pulford to get an answer but he said he had not yet talked to Bill Wirtz, the Blackhawks owner. As the weeks went by I finally told Pulford I need an answer or Cooke would get upset and I'd be out of the Kings job. Finally Pulford told me Mr. Wirtz wanted to hire someone from Cincinnati. I said that's fine, called Cooke and accepted his offer for five more seasons.

THE MAGAZINE

In the mid-1980s before a game in Washington, D.C., a writer told me he was doing an article on Jack Kent Cooke for the *Los Angeles Magazine* and he heard that I had some Cooke stories. He interviewed me and printed the stories I related to him.

About a week after the magazine came out, the author called me and asked, "Did you read the article?" When I said yes, he asked, "Did I quote you correctly?" I again said yes, and he said Cooke was very upset and told him, "Miller was a disgruntled employee and he's spreading lies." I told the writer that everything I told him was true, and he said, "That's good because I'm writing it again for *Washingtonian Magazine.*" At that time Cooke lived in the D.C. area in Virginia.

A few weeks later, I got a call from my former broadcast partner, Dan Avey. He told me Cooke had called him while in Los Angeles and even though Dan had not spoken to Cooke for some 12 years, Cooke didn't say hello or how are you he just started, "Dan, what is Miller up to? He's spreading falsehoods."

Cooke at this time owned the *Los Angeles Daily News* so I decided to call him and talk with him about the articles. I phoned the newspaper and was told that he was leaving California that night, but he would call me back.

The Kings were opening the 1988-89 season that night and were playing games on Thursday, Saturday, and Sunday. By Sunday, I had not heard from Cooke. I had made a list of points I was going to make during our phone call, and since I no longer worked for him, I was determined not to be intimidated.

After the weekend games I was home on Monday morning having almost forgotten about the call to Cooke when the phone rang and the woman said, "Mr. Miller, please hold for Mr. Cooke." I panicked. My notes were upstairs, and I was downstairs.

Cooke came on the phone and bellowed, "You called me!"

I said, "Yes, Mr. Cooke. I understand you're upset over the magazine articles."

He said, "I'm more than upset. I'm mortified, that you would spread such lies… Goodbye."

And he hung up.

A week later I told the story to Kings owner Bruce McNall who got a laugh out of it, and then I said, "Bruce, don't ever sell the team back to Cooke, or I'm the first one to go."

McNALL AND THE MIGHTY DUCKS

During the 1992-93 season the NHL, with Kings owner Bruce McNall as chairman of the Board of Governors, convinced the Disney Company and its chairman, Michael Eisner, to put an expansion team in Anaheim, California. That was a mere 35 miles from the home of the Kings. The price for a new team to join the league was $50 million, and McNall would get half of that as compensation for allowing another team into his territory. In his book, *Fun While It Lasted*, McNall said he received $12.5 million in cash and a note at a low- interest rate for the remainder.

I have always felt that was one of McNall's worst decisions, but as he said in his book, "I needed the money." The Kings were drawing capacity crowds with Wayne Gretzky, and all this did was take some hockey fans away from the Kings and send them to Anaheim. This was the season the Kings went to the Stanley Cup Finals, and without a team in Anaheim the Kings probably would have had a waiting list for season tickets.

My partner, Jim Fox, and I were doing a Kings telecast the day the new team in Anaheim was named. The Disney Company named them after a successful Disney movie, *The Mighty Ducks*. On the air I said to Jim, "Did you hear what they named the new team in Anaheim?" Jim said, "Yes, they'll be called the Mighty Ducks," and I said, "Yes, and as an expansion team they'll also be known as the Dead Ducks, the Lame Ducks, and the Sitting Ducks."

The next day I was out Christmas shopping, and when I returned home, my wife said, "Michael Eisner called and wants you to phone him." I thought she was kidding. I also thought he was either upset over what we had said on the air about his team or he was going to offer me a job. When I called him back, he said, "Bob, thanks for the mention last night. I was watching your telecast, and it was nice of you to talk about us."

I guess the saying is true, any publicity is good publicity.

FIRST
INTERMISSION

THE SHMOOS

After the conclusion of the 1976-77 season my broadcast partner Rich Marotta asked me what we were supposed to do in the off-season.

"I'm not sure," I told him. "But don't go asking anyone or they will come up with a job for us."

I told Rich to stay home and out of sight. A few days later he called me and told me he wasn't comfortable staying home and that he felt he should be working.

I knew it was a question of time before he got us into trouble so I devised a little trouble for us. A few days later I found Rich at the Forum.

"Well now you've done it," I told him. "Mr. Cooke wants us to sell advertising on the shmoos."

"What is a shmoo?" he asked confused.

"They are the waist-high concrete pylons in the parking lot that direct the traffic," I explained with a smile.

"The term *shmoo* came from the *Lil Abner* comic strip in which characters called shmoos kept multiplying."

Rich couldn't believe what I was telling him, but I assured him it was true. We were going to have to peddle the team to every Mom and Pop shop.

"I swear. We have to go up and down Manchester Boulevard and tell merchants they can buy a half a shmoo for $15 or a whole shmoo for $25."

Later that morning I let Kings general manager Jake Milford in on my scheme and that I was having lunch with Rich and his dad at the Forum Club.

Jake, who could put anyone on with a straight face, smiled and said he would join us, so the four of us went out for "working" lunch.

"How is it going, Jake?" I asked, making small talk.

"That Mr. Cooke is driving me crazy. He's on my back about everything ... and you two guys," he complained while pointing to Rich and myself, "when are you going to get started on selling those shmoos?"

"What in the hell is a shmoo?" Rich's dad asked.

Every time we mentioned selling the shmoos Rich's head dropped in despair. He was so depressed for having to do something so demeaning. Jake and I left in high spirits, knowing by the down look on Rich's face that we had hooked him.

After lunch Rich's dad called him.

"I was looking at those shmoos as I drove out of the parking lot," he said. "They're all cracked and chipped. If you ever came into my business and tried to sell me one of those things, I'd kick you right out on the street."

This put Rich into another spasm.

Later I called Rich to come to my office, and I pretended I had the president of Sizzler restaurants on the phone.

"He wants to buy a shmoo," I assured Rich as I handed him a 12-inch ruler. "He wants to know how big they are, so do me a favor and go out to the parking lot and measure one."

He looked at me skeptically, but after I insisted, he trudged off to measure the shmoo. A group of us who were in on the joke hid in the entrance of the Forum to watch Rich. He went to a shmoo, held the ruler at the bottom of the concrete, marked where the top of the ruler ended with his hand, and then used his hand as a base for the next 12 inches. Once he was done, I raced back to my office before he got there.

"They are 36 inches high," he reported.

"Do you know how big around they are?" I asked.

"What? No!" he responded as his face reddened.

Later that night I told my wife the story.

"You should call Rich and tell him it's a joke," she said.

"I'll wait a few days. Let him stew over it a bit."

Well, he did stew over it. Unbeknownst to me, that night Rich called some broadcasting friends of his, Cleve Herman at KFWB and Allin Slate at KNX, and said he had a real crisis and had to talk with them. They picked him up, and on the way to Dodger Stadium for a ballgame they waited for Rich to drop this bombshell.

"Rich, what is this big crisis?" one of them asked.

After a pause Rich told them.

"I have to sell advertising on the shmoos."

"What is a shmoo?" they asked.

When Rich told them, they burst out laughing, which made Rich feel worse. After that Rich met with his dad and Uncle Pete to discuss his dilemma. It went so far that Rich actually composed a letter of resignation to Mr. Cooke, which asked how Mr. Cooke expected him to sell shmoo advertising since he knew nothing about selling advertising or shmoos.

A few days after I started the prank, I called Rich at home to let him in on the joke.

"Rich, you know those shmoos?" I began.

"Yes," he replied despondently.

"Well, I was only kidding," I confessed.

There was silence as he processed the news.

"What?" he shouted.

"I was only kidding about the shmoos."

Silence.

"Oh, I'm so happy," Rich said. "You son of a bitch. …Oh, I am so relieved. … You son of a bitch."

I think we sold him on the prank because even years later Rich and I still laugh about it. And luckily for me, he never sent Mr. Cooke that resignation letter.

4

SECOND PERIOD

JESTER'S TALES IN THE KINGS' COURT

AIRSICKNESS

Pete Weber, my broadcast partner from 1979 to 1981, liked to pull some practical jokes. On an early-morning commercial flight out of Boston, Pete had a window seat, and I was on the aisle of a fully loaded plane. In those years, nearly all teams used commercial flights. A gentleman we didn't know was seated between us. I was reading the morning newspaper as Pete leaned forward and said to me, "Boy, I sure hope I don't get sick like I did on the last flight."

With that, I looked at our fellow passenger, and he had his head down and was shaking it as if to say, "Why me?"

I said to him, "I'd switch seats with you, but the last flight he threw up all over my pants and shoes."

Now the guy was really upset. As we pushed back from the gate, Pete made a big production out of getting the "barf" bag out of the seat pocket and getting it opened. He leaned his head against the window, and all the time we were taxiing, he pretended as if he were going to be sick. By now our friend is trying

71

to be subtle as he peers over the tops of the seats in front of him to see if there is another open seat. There were none.

All that time, I was holding the newspaper over my face because I was laughing so hard. As we started rolling down the runway for takeoff, Pete, louder than I think he meant to, let out a loud sound as if he were vomiting—so loud that a woman with a huge bouffant hairdo seated in front of him let out a scream and threw her arms behind her head envisioning what was coming.

We all had a good laugh, even our unwilling victim in the middle seat.

BOO

One of the funniest incidents at a Kings training camp took place in 1986. The Kings held training camp in Victoria, British Columbia, Canada, and the team was headquartered at the Harbour Towers hotel. The hotel featured balconies outside some rooms, and it was possible, although not easy, to climb from one balcony to the one next door.

It was the night before the end of camp, and curfew was at 10 p.m. Kings players Bernie Nicholls and Phil Sykes decided to climb over to an adjoining balcony on the fifth floor to frighten two French-Canadian junior players who had been invited to camp. Unbeknownst to Nicholls and Sykes, the problem was the two young players had been cut from the roster earlier in the day and sent back to their junior teams.

As Nicholls and Sykes climbed to the balcony of the adjoining room, they found the sliding-glass door open, as it was a pleasant fall night in Victoria. Nicholls was the first to enter the room, bursting through the curtains, racing over to the bed and screaming, "Yaaaaaah!" Right behind him was Sykes who also raced to the bed screaming.

At this point, two elderly women, who now occupied the room, sat bolt upright in bed and also started screaming. Sykes later said, "That scared us out of our minds." They both bolted to the balcony and back to Nicholls' room.

Nicholls' roommate was Kings defenseman Dean Kennedy. The next morning word of the prank got around, and Kings coach Pat Quinn was fuming. At practice, Sykes said Quinn skated the team hard and all the while stood at center ice, with a scowl on his face, slamming the blade of his stick onto the ice. Quinn thought Kennedy was one of the culprits since he roomed with Nicholls. Quinn was so upset at the two players he wouldn't call them by name; he called them by their numbers—No. 9 and No. 6. At the end of practice, Quinn said, "Nine and six, I want to see you." Sykes told No. 6, Dean Kennedy, "I'll go talk to him." Quinn looked at Sykes and said, "What are you doing here?" Sykes said, "Well, I was involved in what I think you want to talk to us about."

Nicholls and Sykes recounted the story, and when they got to the part about the elderly ladies screaming and scaring Nicholls and Sykes, Quinn had to smile. After the incident, the two ladies had called the front desk, and Nicholls and Sykes had to pay for the ladies' room and their incidental expenses. A Kings players' "Kangaroo Court" fined Nicholls and Sykes $500, which was contributed to the players' Halloween party fund.

THE RACE

Practical jokes are a part of any sports team, and the Kings have had their share. On the 1973 Kings team was a player named Don Kozak, who prided himself in maintaining superb physical condition. He and his wife, Tanya, lived in an area of Los Angeles called the Palos Verdes Peninsula and during the summer months Tanya would ride her horse through the hills of Palos Verdes while he ran behind her for miles. He would also run on the beach for several miles a day to get in shape.

One September day at the Victoria training camp, the Kings players decided to pull a joke on Kozak and bet him that goaltender Rogie Vachon could beat him in a race. Vachon, although a tremendous goaltender, was never known for exercising too strenuously. The players all put up phony bets, and the race was on. Behind the Memorial Arena in Victoria was a huge rock—so big that the entire team could stand on it and so high that you couldn't see one side from the other. The race was to consist of 10 laps around the rock. Each runner had a trainer, Real Lemieux was Kozak's trainer; and Gilles Marotte was the trainer for Vachon. All of the players except Kozak were in on the ruse, and Lemieux instructed Kozak to "… take off like a rabbit and Vachon would never catch up."

The Kings had a player on that team named Randy Rota, who was about the same size and build as Vachon. They dressed Rota and Vachon alike, and when the race started, Vachon allowed Kozak to sprint out ahead. When he was out of sight, Vachon left the track and hid in the bushes, and Rota took his place the track. Rota stayed far enough behind that when Kozak looked over his shoulder, he thought it was Vachon. Prior to the final lap, Vachon in the weeds, splashed water on himself, came back on the track, and sprinted to overtake Kozak, who couldn't believe that Rogie had that much stamina left. As Vachon started to pass Kozak in the final turn, Kozy, who was stumbling and exhausted, started grabbing Vachon's shirt and holding him up. Rogie pulled away, however, and won the race, much to the dismay of Kozak. Here he had trained all summer and was in tip-top shape and couldn't even beat Vachon. Kozy was in tears, and the players started paying up their phony bets.

So distraught and exhausted was Kozak that he missed practice that morning; but after a while, the players let him in on the practical joke.

EIGHT INCHES OF SHAFT

Sometimes things you say on the air don't come out the way you intend them to. The night of March 21, 1981, the Kings were playing in Edmonton. At one point in the game, Kings goaltender Mario Lessard broke his stick. A goalie is the only player who can continue to play with a broken stick; and in my excitement calling the play-by-play, I said, "Mario Lessard has broken his stick …" and here's when I realized this was not going to sound right, "… he's standing in front of the net with about eight inches of his shaft in his hand."

My broadcast partner, Pete Weber, was howling, and I later told Mario that I had given him the benefit of the doubt.

PEEING IN PHILLY

At the Spectrum in Philadelphia, the broadcast location was at the top of the upper deck, and no bathroom facilities were available. During the third period of a game on November 3, 1985, I was in trouble. Nature was calling, and I was extremely uncomfortable. The scoreboard clock showed about eight minutes left, which meant in real time about 15 minutes; and we still had a postgame show to do. I realized I couldn't make it that long and that I would have to join a long list of announcers who, during their careers, were forced to use the soft-drink cups to relieve themselves. I knew I couldn't do it during a stoppage in play—if my partner Nick Nickson ever saw me, we would both break up in fits of laughter. As Nick was talking, I lined up the soft-drink cup; and as I did the play-by-play, I started urinating into the cup. A further problem occurred in that one cup was not enough. So I had to stop, lean down, and with my head on the counter, line up another cup, all the while saying, "The face-off is in the Kings zone …" etc.

I managed to pull it off, and only at the end of the game did I tell Nick what I had done. To this day, I'm not sure he believes me.

CONFUSED BUSES, LOST DRIVERS

Team-bus drivers often are the targets of visiting coaches and players. Two such incidents took place in the mid-1970s in Boston, which is an awful place to drive. It's amazing to me how bus drivers and taxi drivers in that city sometimes have no idea of directions.

Kings coach Bob Pulford sat on the bus where most coaches sit—the front seat on the opposite side of the driver. In this instance, it was becoming apparent the driver was not sure how to get to the Boston Garden, so Pulford started giving him directions. In his usual gruff voice Pulford said, "Turn right; now take a left; now turn right again." We ended up with the bus in a dead-end alley. The players were stifling laughs, as they knew Pulford was embarrassed.

The driver slowly turned in his seat to face Pulford and said, "Have you got any other bright ideas?"

Pulford, with his head down, mumbled, "Well, you're on your own now."

As a player and as a Kings coach, Bob Berry took his cue from Pulford on how to berate bus drivers. One late night—again in Boston during his playing career—Berry was seated right behind the driver with a hanging garment bag separating the two. Most of the players were sleeping when it became obvious the second time we circled the Boston Garden, that the driver didn't know the way to the hotel. Soon a voice from the rear of the bus said, "Hey, Bussie, we're going to be in town for two days. We don't need a tour at two in the morning."

Berry was calmly reading a book and soon the players started egging him on. Defenseman Bob Murdoch was yelling, "Hey, Bobby Berry, are you okay? Are you sick? Hey, Berry, we're lost. Are you sleeping?"

All the while Berry just smiled to himself, said nothing, and kept reading.

Finally, the driver found the hotel; and as he pulled up in front and stopped the bus, Berry calmly pulled the garment bag aside and said to the driver, "You f——-ing dummy."

The players broke up laughing.

***

One bus driver who captured the support of the Kings players was a young black man in Detroit named Wade.

The year was 1975 and the Kings had played in Pittsburgh on November 22 and lost 6-3. Immediately after the game, they flew to Detroit, arriving at about 1 a.m. and not in a good mood. Usually the driver simply starts driving, but this night the driver stood up in of the bus and said, "Gentlemens, welcome to Detroit. My name is Wade, and I'll be your driver during your stay here." At this point, the annoyed players hollered, "Just drive the bus." Wade smiled and as he started to pull away, he happened to grind the gears as he shifted. All the players started laughing, and so did Wade.

The game in Detroit on November 23 was Marcel Dionne's first appearance back in Detroit against the team he left to join the Kings. A raucous standing-room-only crowd of 14,565 filled the old Olympia Stadium. They hung derisive banners and booed Dionne all night long. Fans behind the Kings bench threw programs and paper cups filled with beer and soft drinks at Kings coach Bob Pulford. Pulford and Kings players almost went into the stands after a couple of fans; and police even ejected one fan. Detroit won the game 4-1.

Olympia Stadium had a lobby area where players could greet family and friends after the game. That night police informed the Kings that no one in the Kings party would be allowed into the lobby due to security problems. All team personnel were told to leave the locker room through a back door leading to the parking lot. The team bus pulled up close enough to the door so that when the bus doors were opened, no one could get past the bus doors to the locker-room door as hundreds of unruly fans were mulling over a riot in the parking lot.

As the Kings' bus started to pull away, two crazed, drunken Red Wings fans defiantly stood about 20 feet away in front of the bus. Wade floored the gas pedal and went right at the two, who leaped out of the way. The players were now cheering Wade with shouts of "Way to go, Wade!" and "Let's hear it for Wade!"

Wade made a lot of friends on that Kings team.

REBECCA CARBINO

One night in the mid-1990s, the Kings were in Hartford to play the Whalers. In the game notes, the national anthem singer is always identified, and this night the notes said the singer would be Rebecca Carbino. Our television producer told me when to announce the anthem, and I said, "Now, ladies and gentlemen, from Hartford, Connecticut, here is Rebecca Carbino with our national anthem."

As I looked down on the ice, I saw a 6-foot-5, heavyset black man making his way on the ice to sing the anthem. He had a beautiful, deep voice and did a superb job. Usually, my partner, Jim Fox, is the first one to speak on the air following the anthem, but this night, all during the anthem, he was laughing and pointing at me as if to say, "You've got to get yourself out of this one."

When the anthem was over and we came back on the air, I said, "Ladies and gentlemen, I'm not from Hartford—and I don't know Rebecca Carbino—but that was *not* her."

TWO WEEKS

The Kings had a disastrous season in 1983-84, winning just 23 games, good for a mere 59 points and fifth place in the Smythe Division.

The frustration for me reached its peak in late February. On February 28, the Kings were embarrassed in Calgary 9-1. They were in the midst of a 10-game losing streak. Ten games later, on March 17 in Edmonton, the Kings trailed the Oilers 8-1 when Edmonton's Glenn Anderson scored with 1:45 left in the game and I disgustedly said on the air, "It's now 9 to 1. I haven't seen the Kings play this bad in, oh … two weeks."

My partner, Nick Nickson, howled with laughter. He said he thought I was going to say something like 20 years, not two weeks. Nick left the booth, and I could hear him howling out in the hallway. I could barely speak due to laughing. There was no play-by-play for about the final 90 seconds of the game.

ROOM SERVICE, ANYONE?

At the 1974 NHL All-Star Game in Chicago, Dan Avey pulled a practical joke on Kings publicity director Mike Hope. We were staying at the Palmer House hotel in downtown Chicago; and when we checked in, Avey switched the rooms of general manager Jake Milford and Hope. Hope got the suite intended for Milford, and Milford got the tiny room reserved for Hope. Avey then called the hotel catering service and ordered two plates of hors d'oeuvres, including chocolate-covered strawberries, to be sent to Hope's suite. Hope was under the impression that all this was free—compliments of the hotel. He called me and said, "You've got to come here and see my room; and the hotel is sending me free food."

Hope was on the trip to help legendary *Los Angeles Times* columnist, Jim Murray, who wanted to interview the Blackhawks' Stan Mikita. Soon, we had a roomful of people in Hope's suite enjoying the food and drinks.

Milford arrived all upset because Hope had a bigger room than he did, not aware that Avey had switched the rooms. Milford complained his room was so small he had to go into the hallway just to change his mind. All this time, Avey was calling room service to send up more food. Some of us were in on the prank, and we were enjoying that Hope was thinking how wonderful it was that he was receiving this type of hospitality from the hotel.

Avey approved the hotel bills in those days so everything was handled without Jack Kent Cooke's knowledge.

HAWAIIAN REWARDS

In 1980-81, the Kings had their third-best season in team history with 99 points. Coach Bob Berry led the Kings to 43 wins and second place in the Norris Division, and fourth best in the NHL overall.

Late in February, owner Jerry Buss promised the Kings he would take the players, their families, and other members of the organization to Hawaii after the playoffs. Well the playoffs had a quick and disappointing end as the Kings lost 3-1 in a best-of-five series with the New York Rangers. The final game was a 10-3 rout in New York. Yet, the Kings were off to Hawaii.

Hours before the plane left, the Kings announced that coach Bob Berry had signed a new contract. A couple of days later in Honolulu, Berry had second thoughts and resigned. Later that summer, he signed as head coach with Montreal, and some felt he had sought that job before the Kings left on the trip.

While staying at the Hilton Hawaiian Village in Honolulu, many of the players and personnel would gather on the beach at Waikiki each morning after breakfast. One morning, Captain Dave Lewis was reading the scores in the morning sports section. All of a sudden, he stopped and said, "Holy cow, some stoops are still playing." Of course, the successful teams were still battling for the Stanley Cup while the Kings relaxed in Hawaii.

HOPE AND BROWN

When I joined the Kings in August 1973, the publicity director for the team was an energetic, feisty little guy named Mike Hope. He was a bundle of energy, jumped right into the job, and wasn't afraid to let his opinions be known to anyone—including owner Jack Kent Cooke or the team's general manager or players.

The Kings had a defenseman in those years named Larry Brown, and Larry's wife, Jeanne, was also his agent. Whenever Larry would get injured in a game, Jeanne would run down to the dressing room to check on the seriousness of the injury. Kings general manager Jake Milford told Hope that he didn't want any wives in the dressing room.

One game, Larry got injured, and Jeanne raced downstairs and entered the locker room. Hope told her she was not welcome and took her by the arm and ushered her out. She was not happy about this situation.

After the second period of that game, Hope and Jeanne met again at the landing of a narrow stairway leading down to the locker room. Hope said to her, "I've told you a dozen times, you can't go into the locker room."

Jeanne replied, "You can't tell me what to do."

Hope said, "I'll have security throw you out."

With that Jeanne hauled off and slapped Hope in the face. Not one to back down, Hope slapped her in the face right back. She started crying, and Hope thought he had gone too far. He went up to find Milford and tell him what had happened, thinking he would be fired. Upon hearing the story, Milford said, "Good ... Larry should have done that a long time ago."

STREAKS OF THE STRANGE

In 1974, the "streaking" craze was prevalent, and the Kings were not to be left out. Before a game with the Pittsburgh Penguins at the Forum on March 13, Bryant Gumbel, then a young sportscaster at Channel 4 (KNBC) in Los Angeles, informed me he heard there would be a streaker on the ice some time that night.

I was in the broadcast booth about half an hour before the teams came out for warm-ups, and sure enough, a young lady came onto the ice where the visiting team enters. She was wearing nothing but a pair of sneakers and was holding a Kings pennant above her head. The crowd was startled at first but then cheered as she ran the length of the ice, exited where the Kings enter, jumped into a waiting car in the tunnel, and was whisked away. We found out later she was a stripper named "Miss Cindy" and that Kings owner Jack Kent Cooke, always looking for publicity, had approved paying her $100 to streak.

***

One other night, March 5, 1988, at the Forum, someone threw a live chicken on the ice in the first period as the game was in progress. The chicken had what looked like a blue cloth napkin on its back, and it was so scared it remained motionless as it soiled the ice. To my disbelief, play continued for about 30 seconds; and Kings players were skating and stick-handling around the chicken until the referee stopped play. Finally the chicken was removed.

***

Prior to the start of each NHL game, the public address announcer warns spectators to be alert because the puck can fly into the stands and cause injury. One night at the Forum, to my left, a hard slap shot was fired just over the glass and into the crowd. I saw a woman grab her head with both hands, and

I thought she had been hit in the forehead and injured. At that point, however, all the fans seated near her started laughing.

It so happened the woman was wearing a wig, and the puck had picked the wig off her head and knocked it about eight rows behind her. She was covering her hair in embarrassment while the crowd passed the wig down the rows back to her.

VEGAS ICE

Usually the only thing to get excited about in the preseason is that it signals the regular season is near, but it's also a chance to see some young prospects in game situations. The Kings changed that in 1991, when they uniquely scheduled an outdoor game at Caesar's Palace in Las Vegas against the New York Rangers.

The game was played on a portable ice rink set up in the parking lot behind the hotel, where boxing matches were held. To shield the ice from the sun, netting held up by ropes was positioned about 10 feet above the ice. At 1 p.m. on game day, workmen removing the net accidentally dropped it on the ice, and the heated ropes melted into the ice causing hundreds of ripples on the surface. Then, about 1:30, it rained for half an hour.

At 4:30, I walked to the rink and watched a maintenance man squeegee about an inch of water off the ice. I thought, "There is no way a game will be played tonight." Fortunately, the portable ice is quite thick, and the Zamboni machine was able to scrape off the ripples and reflood the ice as the temperature was dropped. Sure enough, by 7:30 that night, 13,007 fans, all decked out in various NHL team jerseys, were ready for the opening face-off with the temperature at 85 degrees.

Kings goalie Kelly Hrudey consented—and so did the NHL—to have a tiny television camera taped to the side of his helmet. We called it the "Hrudey Cam," and it may have been the first point-of-view camera used in hockey. It was supposed to give the television viewer the same perspective of the play as the goalie. At one point, one of the officials skated toward Hrudey, looked at his helmet, and mouthed the words "Hi, Mom!" into the camera.

Another problem that night was grasshoppers. Attracted by the bright lights, they were all over the ice. They were about an inch and a half long, and players would cut them in half as they skated over them.

The Kings won the game 5-2, and the fans had a great time at the game and in the casinos. The next day, the Kings flew all the way across country to Charlotte, North Carolina, to play the Rangers on September 29, but the portable ice at the Charlotte Coliseum was chipping, and the game was cancelled due to the poor ice conditions.

HOT NEWS

One Sunday morning in 1974, when the Kings' charter bus was leaving the Vancouver airport, Don Kozak was sitting in front of Kings radio and television-color commentator Dan Avey, engrossed in reading the newspaper. Kozak had pulled out one section and left the rest of the paper in the aisle between his seat and the seat of Kings trainer Pete Demers. While Kozak caught up on the news, Avey took a matchbook from his pocket, got out a match, and lit it. As quick as lightning Avey reached between the seats and set the bottom edge of Kozak's paper on fire. The little flame grew and began spitting out smoke, but Kozak was so wrapped up in his reading that he didn't notice.

A few moments later, his eyes zeroed in on the flames and the smoke; and he tossed the paper across the aisle and onto Demers' head. Demers, who is jittery even in the best of times, let out this blood-curdling scream and dropped the section where the rest of the Sunday paper sat, setting it ablaze, and ran to the front of the bus. The fire grew, reaching the armrests as the furious driver pulled to the side of the road and searched for the key to unlock the fire extinguisher. I wasn't going to stand around;

I got off the bus and waited with assistant trainer John Holmes on the side of the road.

Back on the bus, Avey, who started the whole escapade, jumped on the paper and stomped the fire out with his feet.

Meanwhile, Holmes and I were enjoying a smoke-free environment when Coach Bob Pulford leaned out of the door.

"Get the hell back in the bus," he ordered gruffly.

"Pully, the bus is on fire," I stated. "I think I'll stand out here if you don't mind."

As we returned to our seats, I heard the team laughing hysterically. The driver got up in the front of the bus and began to chew them out.

"You think this is a joke," he ranted. "You call yourselves professionals. There's going to be a bill for the fire damage to this vehicle."

The players were less than sympathetic.

"Sit down and drive the f---ing bus," one of them hollered.

I wish I could say that was a one-time incident. However, on February 28, 1977, we had another hot news flash in Buffalo. The Kings had played the Sabres the night before, and we were headed to the airport for an early-morning flight to Washington D.C. It was about 6:00 a.m., and all was quiet with most of the players and personnel asleep.

All of a sudden, goaltender Rogie Vachon began yelling from the back, in his French-Canadian accent, "Stop de bus! Stop de bus!"

When I looked back there, the entire back of the bus was red with flames. The driver pulled over and was steaming mad. Before he got back there, someone had stomped out another newspaper fire.

"Y-y-you g-g-guys t-t-think t-t-this is f-f-funny?" he stuttered from the front of the bus. "Y-y-you c-c-call y-y-yourselves p-p-professionals."

And once again, one of the players responded.

"Just drive the f---ing bus."

He dropped us off and all of the team—except Coach Pulford—continued to the terminal. Once we got there, I waited to speak to the coach. After a very long time, he finally showed up.

"What took you so long?"

"The driver swore he would not pick us up for the game next week," Pulford answered. We were playing Buffalo a few days later to make up a cancelled game. "It took some tickets to the game and a promise that no one would set his bus on fire to change his mind."

I just shook my head and hoped that Pulford could make sure that he'd uphold his end of the bargain.

SNOW IN ST. LOUIS

You would expect snow to be a problem in Buffalo, New York, but not in St. Louis. On December 19, 1973, the Kings were in St. Louis to play the Blues, but a snowstorm held the crowd to only 4,115.

We were doing our radio pregame show when I heard a public address announcement. I had earphones on and couldn't make out the announcement, but all of a sudden, the fans started rushing for the exits. I thought to myself, "Maybe the announcer said the building was on fire." When we broke for a commercial, I asked our engineer what the announcement was to the crowd. He said they told fans that since they had made an effort to battle the storm and attend the game, there would be free beer and hot dogs at the concession stands.

The next morning, the Kings were to fly home, but due to the storm, all flights were cancelled or delayed. In those days, the radio-television color commentator, Dan Avey, also handled the team travel arrangements. While Dan manned the phones at the hotel looking for a flight, I headed for the airport about 9 a.m.

We didn't get out of St. Louis until 6 p.m. that night, so I spent all day in the TWA lounge. I struck up a conversation with a gentleman who said he was trying to get to Anaheim, California, for a concert. I asked his name, and he said, "I'm Tex Beneke, the leader of the Glenn Miller orchestra."

CALGARY TOWER

At the start of the 1990 playoffs in Calgary, I received a phone call one morning from Bob Borgen, our television feature producer. He said, "How would you like to do a feature from the top of the Calgary Tower?"

The Calgary Tower is a 625-foot-high landmark in downtown Calgary with a restaurant and observation deck on top. I said, "You mean in the restaurant?" and he replied, "No, I mean out on the roof of the tower."

He told me I would be hooked to a safety belt, but then he added—jokingly, I hoped—"If you fall to your death, your family will receive free season tickets to the Flames games."

I thought it might be fun, so I agreed. I signed a release with Tower management and climbed through a trap door out onto the roof, looking straight down to the street some 625 feet below. The roof was slanted toward the outside edge, so I walked on a slight incline uphill toward a television antenna in the middle of the roof. At this point, I saw a television cameraman setting up his tripod.

I did a commentary on the series, which featured the Kings against the defending Stanley Cup Champion Calgary Flames. Borgen then said for me to remain on top of the Tower until he and the camera crew could drive to the far side of the Saddledome. With a zoom lens, they'd get a shot toward the arena, then over the arena to the top of the tower. At that point, they would flash the headlights on their van, and I would then raise a Kings pennant over my head to signify the Kings were on top of Calgary.

The following day, Randy Hahn, who was the third announcer on our crew and who did the between-periods features, was

Bob Miller and television producer Bob Borgen on top of the 625-foot Calgary (Alberta) Tower. *PHOTO COURTESY OF BOB BORGEN*

out with a television crew at the Calgary Olympic ski-jump site. As a joke, with the crew taping, Randy went to a high-powered binocular stand and looked through the binoculars, then turned toward the camera and said, "Wow, some asshole is standing on top of the Calgary Tower." At that point, they were going to cut to me with the pennant above my head. Fortunately, that portion never got on the air.

PEA IN THE WHISTLE

Many times during a telecast, an announcer may say something that causes fits of laughter with no one able to speak. That happened during our telecast of the Kings-Florida Panthers game at Staples Center on December 1, 2011.

With 13:53 left in the first period and a faceoff coming up in the Florida zone, my partner Jim Fox said, on the air, "Bob, there's going to be a delay because something is wrong with linesman Don Henderson." Henderson had skated over to the Florida bench and had his back to our TV location. We speculated that perhaps he was injured. Seconds later, he turned and we could see that he had a new whistle, and on the air Jim said, "Oh, I see, the pea in his whistle wasn't moving," to which I said on the air, "Hey, a lot of us have had that problem." We immediately broke into fits of laughter, and neither of us could speak. Jim darted to the back of our broadcast booth, and I could hear him laughing.

I thought I had regained my composure and started to describe the play by play again but got only a few words out of my mouth before I broke up again.

In seconds, in this time of social media, our blooper went all over the country.

SECOND INTERMISSION

GEORGE MAGUIRE

George Maguire, the Kings general manager from 1977 to 1983 was a stocky, florid-faced Canadian. He liked to drink a little—or perhaps a lot—and he was an individual who was not happy unless he was upset about something, and the smallest thing could put him in a bad mood. Come to think of it, most of the time he was in a bad mood. He could be belligerent, quarrelsome, combative, coarse, caustic, vulgar, crude, rude, and uncouth—and that was on a good day. I think that just about sums him up. If you need a visual image, just think of the late Australian actor Leo McKern as Horace Rumpole in the English television series *Rumpole of the Bailey.*

He spent 26 years in the Canadian Military, which I think helped shape his personality. He spent years as a scout for the Montreal Canadiens, the Boston Bruins, and the Minnesota North Stars; and as the Chief Scout for the Kings, and he was extremely efficient in that role. When the Kings had traded away most of their high draft picks in the early years, Maguire found some outstanding players that other teams had overlooked, such as Butch Goring (drafted 51st); Neil Komadoski (48th); Dave Hutchison (36th), Gary Sargent (48th), Dave Taylor (210th), and Hall of Fame goalie Billy Smith (59th).

He was brought to L.A. to be assistant general manager to Jake Milford. Owner Jack Kent Cooke had this penchant for pitting two executives against each other until one of them quit; I never understood this type of management. In the summer of 1977, both Milford and head coach Bob Pulford resigned because neither of them could get along with Cooke or with Maguire, who then was named general manager.

I never realized how crazy things could get in professional sports until one night before a home game: Maguire came to my office and told me and my broadcast partner, Rich Marotta, not to mention the name of Bob Murdoch. Murdoch was a Kings defenseman. I asked Maguire, "Why isn't he playing?" Maguire said, "Well, he is playing."

I said, "Murdoch is playing, but you don't want me to mention his name? What am I supposed to say on the air, 'Folks, I know who has the puck, but I can't tell you'?"

Then George made one of the most unbelievable statements ever, as he said, "I don't know, but I'll tell you one thing: this honesty bullshit has got to stop."

Maguire didn't want Murdoch's name mentioned because Mr. Cooke had moved to Nevada due to his divorce proceeding and would listen to the game on radio. Cooke didn't like Murdoch, and each time he would hear me mention Murdoch's name on the broadcast, Cooke would phone George and give him hell. As I recall, that night Murdoch had a great game, blocking shots, making great defensive plays, and even scoring a goal. Each time I would I would say, "What a great play by Murdoch," I would look at George, and he'd be pounding his fist on the counter.

***

Maguire sat in the front row of the press box about four seats to my right. He could hear us doing the play-by-play. One night on the air, I said to my partner, Pete Weber, "I don't see Butch Goring on the ice or on the bench. Do we have any report that he's injured?" "No I haven't heard about any injury," Pete said. George heard this, and being oblivious to live microphones, he leaned over toward us and said, "Butch Goring's got a boil on his arse—that's why he's not playing." Nothing like our audience getting an up-to-the-minute injury report.

***

In many of the Maguire years, Kings attendance was down. On many nights, the Forum was only half-full. One night the Kings goaltender broke his stick and the Kings iced the puck to get a whistle. When play stopped, the building was quiet, and I heard a fan about two sections over to my right holler, "Hey, Maguire. I didn't pay 10 bucks to see this team ice the puck all night." I looked at George, and he was fuming—his face looked like a thermometer getting redder and redder. George then turned in his seat, looked toward where the voice had come from, and hollered back, "What do you want him to do, play goal with his pecker?"

Two sections of fans broke up laughing.

***

There was a female Kings fan who would be half-soused by the end of the first period. She would then follow Maguire through the crowd as he walked toward the stairway to go down to his office. She would be taunting him, "This team stinks; when are they going to win?" or "I'm a season-ticket holder; when are you going to get some good players?" Finally, one night George had

had enough. He whirled around and shouted at her, "You can shove your season tickets right up your arse."

"Wonderful, we are having trouble drawing fans, and the GM is insulting them," I thought.

***

At another game, several people in the press box noticed a couple seated in the upper reaches of the Forum known as the colonnade. This couple was getting more and more amorous, and soon most everyone in the press box was following the action—and I don't mean on the ice. Someone pointed out to George what was going on and George said, "Jesus Christ, you'd think if the guy was going to get laid, he'd buy a higher priced seat."

5

THE KINGDOM

PAID INTERVIEWS

On January 14, 1979, the Kings were in Boston to play the Bruins. In the Boston Garden, the radio-television location was on one side of the ice, and the print media were on the opposite side. I wanted to interview Kings GM George Maguire between periods on our telecast. I saw George across the ice in the press box, so I called the Bruins media relations director, Nate Greenberg. I asked Nate to ask George if he would join us at the end of the first period. Nate called back and said George refused. I didn't think much of it since I figured he was going to meet with Bruins GM Harry Sinden between periods.

The next morning, as we checked in at Boston's Logan airport, Maguire said to me in a belligerent voice, "What would prompt you to make that request last night?" I thought he meant, "Why didn't you ask me yourself instead of having Nate Greenberg do it?"

I told him I wanted to ask him myself but didn't see him until after I had arrived in our broadcast location. George said, "That isn't what I mean."

I said, "Well, what do you mean?"

"I don't get $500 from Zenith," he answered. "Why would I go on with you?" In those days, our players received $500 to put toward merchandise from Zenith for appearing as guests on our telecasts. I couldn't believe my ears. I was very upset, and I said, "That's a horseshit attitude by our general manager that you need to be paid to go on our telecast."

Now George was upset, and as I walked away, he was shouting, "What do you mean, 'it's a horseshit attitude?'" blah, blah, blah. I then told my partner, Pete Weber, "We will never interview Maguire again, I don't care what happens." And we didn't.

By this time, former Kings general manager Jake Milford was the general manager of the Vancouver Canucks. Whenever the Canucks would play the Kings in L.A., we would interview Jake between periods, but we would never interview Maguire. When the interview was over, Milford would stand behind Maguire and say in a loud voice to me, "Bob, what do I get for being on with you?," and then he would wink at me.

I'd say, loud enough for Maguire to hear, "You get two tailor-made suits from a clothier on Wilshire Boulevard."

Milford would then ask Maguire, "Is that what I get for being on the air?"

Maguire would answer, "Don't ask me. Those two bastards never put me on the air."

All of us—except George—would get a big laugh.

THE MONKEY AND THE ORGAN GRINDER

Probably one of the funniest lines ever uttered in a courtroom occurred during the 1978 off-season. That year, the Detroit Red Wings signed Kings goaltender Rogie Vachon as a free agent, and as compensation, the Kings received Detroit forward Dale McCourt. McCourt had a very good rookie year with Detroit, however, and didn't want to leave the team; so he and then-Red Wings GM Ted Lindsay challenged the deal and went to court to block it.

During the court hearing, Kings GM George Maguire took the stand and said about Detroit, "They shouldn't have messed with my goalie." McCourt's attorney asked Maguire why he didn't make an offer to Vachon, to which Maguire replied, "I did, but I made it to his agent."

The attorney then asked, "Why didn't you make the offer to Mr. Vachon?"

"Why would I talk to the monkey when I can talk to the organ grinder?" Maguire responded.

Al Coates was Detroit's public-relations director at that time, and he said the courtroom exploded in laughter upon hearing Maguire's response. Some observers ran out of the room in hysterics, and the court had to call a recess.

When everything was worked out—a year later—McCourt stayed with Detroit, and the Kings were awarded forward Andre St. Laurent and two No. 1 draft picks from the Red Wings as compensation for their signing Vachon.

With those two No. 1 picks, the Kings drafted defenseman Larry Murphy in 1980 and forward Doug Smith in 1981.

A LITTLE PR

In 1983, the Kings decided to hold training camp in Los Angeles instead of going to some distant locale as they had done in the past. The plan was to make the team more accessible to local reporters so they could stir publicity on the upcoming season. The camp would be held at the Kings practice rink in Culver City, and on the first day of camp, the temperature was about 103 degrees. Overnight, one of the compressors, which keeps the ice frozen, broke down; so when the players and media arrived for the first practice session, the ice was almost completely melted. A quick call was made to George Maguire, who was steaming mad when he arrived at the rink. As he stormed into the building, reporter Sam McManus, of the *Los Angeles Times*, who had been assigned to cover the Kings, said to George, "Can I ask you a question?"

George whirled around and said, "Get away from me, you're a goddamn pest."

This was on the first day—so much for media relations.

***

During a team commercial flight one season, I was seated on the plane when Maguire arrived a little late. He was huffing and puffing, sweating and red in the face as he walked down the aisle struggling with his luggage. I could tell he was in his usual bad mood. Just then, one of the female flight attendants said to him in a cheery voice, "May I take your garment bag, sir?"

George turned and said to her, "You can shove my garment bag right up your arse."

What a wonderful representative of the team.

***

In the Stanley Cup playoffs of 1980, the Kings met the New York Islanders with the series starting on Long Island. Maguire did not accompany the team but flew to New York a day later with the team physician, Dr. Vince Carter. As they were seated in the first-class section, the flight attendant asked what they would like to drink. George said, "I'll have a cocktail," and Dr. Carter said, "I'll have orange juice."

With that, Maguire hollered at Dr. Carter, "Why the hell are you flying first class if you're not going to drink?"

WHO SAID KINGS QUIT?

On November 4, 1978, the New York Rangers played in L.A. and soundly beat the Kings 7-3. I was sitting in the press lounge after the game when George Maguire stormed through on the way to his office. I always enjoyed getting George upset—something that was easy to do—so I looked at him and rolled my eyes in disgust over the Kings' performance.

He said to me, "Get Pluto and bring your tape recorder into my office."

For some unknown reason George always called my partner Pete Weber by cartoon names such as Pluto, Bulldog, and Felix. When we arrived in George's office, he said, "Which one of you said the Kings quit? The game was so bad I couldn't bear to watch, so I came to my office and heard one of you say it looks as if the Kings have quit."

I told him I never said that—nor would I *ever* say that—and Pete said he hadn't said anything like that either.

With that, George pointed at a speaker in the ceiling and asked, "Whose voice comes out of that?"

I told him ours did, and he said, "It was right after the Rangers' seventh goal, so play it on your tape recorder."

I played the tape, and there was no reference to the Kings quitting.

George then said, "Well, one of you said it, and I'd better not ever hear it again."

At this point, I was getting upset and said, "I told you neither one of us said anything about the team quitting."

On the drive home, I wondered who would make a statement like that, and I decided it would probably be the opponent's announcers. The next day, I phoned Maguire's assistant, John Wolf, and asked him to listen to the Rangers videotape of the game to see if he heard that statement.

He called me back and said, "Yes, right after the Rangers' seventh goal, Bill Chadwick, the Rangers color announcer, said, 'It looks as if the Kings have quit.'"

I told John to save the tape. When I arrived at the Forum that day, I called George to the video room because I had something to show him. He asked if it was a horror show, and I said, "Yes, last night's game." When I played the tape, George said, "Yep, that's what I heard."

I then waited for him to say he was sorry for accusing Pete and me. When I heard nothing I said, "George, I think you owe Pete and me an apology for that childish outburst in your office last night."

I wondered if I had gone too far and overstepped my bounds. He stared at me, puffing his cigar, his face getting bright red, and then he shouted, "Well, I *apologize*. What do you think I am, a goddamn Canadian diplomat?"

"George," I said, "that's one thing I know you're not."

TRADE WITH RANGERS

On March 14, 1996, the Kings made a significant trade with the New York Rangers. The Kings sent Marty McSorley, Jari Kurri, and Shane Churla to New York in exchange for Mattias Norstrom, Ian Laperriere, and Ray Ferraro.

The general manager who made the deal was Sam McMaster. One of the Kings scouts phoned McMaster's home and spoke to his wife, Colleen, who didn't follow the team's transactions too closely. Sam wasn't home, so the scout said he had heard the Kings had made a trade that day and asked Colleen whom they acquired.

Colleen said, "I can't remember exactly, but I think we got a department store [Norstrom], a water [Laperriere], and a sports car [Ferraro]."

PEEPHOLE

When Bob Berry was the Kings head coach in the late 1970s and early 1980s, we would stay in a hotel near the St. Louis airport when in town to play the Blues. One night Bob and I headed to the hotel's bar on the top floor. As we were seated at the bar, we noticed many "ladies of the night" in attendance. After a while, Berry decided it was time to call it a night.

"I'm tired," he explained. "I'm going to my room."

"Okay, I am going to stay and finish my beer," I told him.

Shortly after Bob had left, one of the ladies came up to me.

"Hi, are you staying in the hotel?" she purred.

"Yes."

"What's your room number?"

I can honestly say that I picked a room number, not my own, out of thin air.

"I'll see you later," she promised. "My name is Cindy."

When I returned to my room, I wondered if I had given her the room number of anyone with the Kings, so I checked the rooming list. Oh boy, I had given her Berry's room number. The next morning as I boarded the bus to go to the arena for the morning skate, I found Bob.

"Good morning," I said. "How are you?"

"Horseshit," he replied. "You know how tired I was when I left you last night. Well, I took a hot bath and went to bed, and at 2 a.m. someone was pounding on my door."

"Who was it?" I asked, feigning concern.

"Some hooker. She said, 'It's Cindy.' And I said, 'Who?' And she said, 'I met you upstairs.' I said, 'I didn't meet anybody upstairs. Go away!' She replied, 'Yeah, you did. Look tru da peephole, look tru da peephole.' She had her face in front of the peephole in the door. I told her to get the hell out."

"Boy, that's too bad," I muttered as I bit my cheek to keep from laughing. "Did you ever get back to sleep?"

I kept my mouth shut about the entire mishap for a couple of months until we came back to St. Louis, the same hotel, and the same hotel bar.

"I have a confession to make to you," I told him as I looked at my beer.

The second I said those words he knew exactly what I was about to say.

"You son of a bitch," he seethed, "you sent her to my room."

To this day, I don't think he believes me when I tell him I didn't know it was his room number when I gave it to Cindy.

PULFORD

Hall of Famer, Bob Pulford played 16 years in the NHL—14 of those with the Toronto Maple Leafs, where he was a member of four Stanley Cup-winning teams and the last two of his career with the Los Angeles Kings. He was named head coach of the Kings at the start of the 1972-73 season. He had a dour personality around most people, especially the players, but was a more gregarious person once you came to know him and he came to know you. I asked him once why he was always so stern around the players, and he said, "Because I never want them to think I'm not serious about this game."

On January 15, 1974, the Kings were in Montreal to play a great Canadiens team. The Forum in Montreal was a tough place to play, and the success of the team called "The Flying Frenchmen" made it even tougher. That particular game, the Kings were winning 2-1 in the third period when the Kings' Frank St. Marseille was called for a tripping penalty with 9:13 left in the game. At the same time, Montreal challenged the legality of the stick of Kings goalie Rogie Vachon. Rogie's stick blade was too wide—it had come from the factory that way—so the Kings received another penalty from referee Wally Harris, and the stick boy was told to get Vachon another stick.

Pulford, upset over the situation, followed the boy into the Kings locker room, locked the door, and said, "Sit down and relax. I'm going to have a cigarette."

Meanwhile, in the arena, none of us knew what the delay was; and as the minutes went by, players from both teams came back on the ice to skate and warm up. At this time, the officials were pounding on the Kings' locker-room door, telling Pulford to get the new stick out there and get the game going. Pulford told them he was trying to cut the stick down to the proper size, but the exasperated officials told him to just play with it the way it was.

Pulford's ploy had worked. The Canadiens had lost their momentum. The Kings killed the penalty two men short for two minutes and won the game.

***

On October 10, 1976, the Kings were in Philadelphia to play another fight-filled game with the Flyers, also known as "The Broad Street Bullies." At 16:56 of the first period, a bench-clearing brawl broke out and delayed the game for 21 minutes. During the brawl, an incensed Pulford grabbed linesman John Brown and was shaking him.

All of a sudden Pulford thought, "What am I doing grabbing an official? I'm in real trouble." So then he started smoothing out the linesman's shirt. Pulford was ejected, becoming the first NHL coach to be ejected from a game since Toe Blake of Montreal was ejected on December 13, 1967, in Boston. The league fined Pulford an "exorbitant" amount of $350. Pulford had no assistant coaches in those days, so general manager Jake Milford took over behind the bench. The Flyers won the game 1-0.

The referees gave 127 minutes in penalties in the first period, and a second bench-clearing brawl took place in the second period. The NHL assessed $9,750 in fines to the two teams.

***

Pulford's wife, Roslyn, should be credited for a rule that now appears in the NHL rulebook. One day she asked her husband, "When you pull the goalie for an extra attacker, why not have him place his stick across the mouth of the goal; since most empty-net goals are scored on shots where the puck stays down on the ice?"

So in Philadelphia one night, Pulford told goalie Rogie Vachon to leave his stick across the empty net if he was pulled from the game. When the time came, Vachon was trying to break his stick and leave it, but he couldn't break it, so he left the entire stick in front of the goal. Pulford said players on the Flyers bench were going wild, screaming, "That's illegal!" at the referee.

There was no rule against it at that time, but it is now deemed illegal.

NEILSON

In the 1983-84 season, Don Perry was fired as Kings head coach after winning only 14 of 50 games, and after general manager Rogie Vachon coached two games in the interim, the Kings hired Roger Neilson as head coach on January 30, 1984. Neilson had coached Vancouver earlier that season and thus became the second man in history to be head coach of two NHL teams in the same season. Fred Glover was the first at Oakland and L.A. in 1971-72.

Neilson was known as "Captain Video" because he was the first NHL coach to rely on videotape as a coaching tool. While with the Kings he told me one of the funniest stories and one of the funniest lines I've ever heard from a coach.

While coaching junior hockey at Peterborough, Ontario, his team played the Sault Ste. Marie Greyhounds and were beaten soundly, something like 9-1. The Greyhounds had a mechanical dog at the roof of the building, and every time they would score, someone would release a lever and the dog would go yelping across the arena. Roger said, "We were sick and tired of hearing that dog, so the next time we played there we went to a hardware store and got some chain, a padlock, and some grease. We got into the arena the night before the game, chained and padlocked the dog, and then spread grease on the ladder leading to the dog."

Then Roger had the greatest line I've ever heard from a coach. He said, "That night, we could hardly wait for them to score."

When the Greyhounds did score, an attendant pulled the lever, and the dog vibrated but couldn't move. The attendant then slid down the greased ladder as he tried to get to the dog. "We were losing," Roger said, "but we were in stitches laughing on the bench."

QUINN AFFAIR

One of the most bizarre situations in NHL history involved the Kings and their coach Pat Quinn in the 1986-87 season. On December 22, 1986, the Kings played an early evening game in Calgary. At dinner after the game, the Kings' Marcel Dionne got a call from a Vancouver radio station asking him what he knew about Kings coach Pat Quinn agreeing to become the general manager of the Vancouver Canucks. Dionne knew nothing about it, which is unusual, because Marcel was usually up to date on the "scoops" around the league.

Later that night in the hotel, the door to my room was open as Quinn passed.

"Should I congratulate you now or later?" I asked.

He laughed it off but later made this statement to the media, "I have a moral and legal obligation to the Kings. I'm not going anywhere."

The following night, the Kings played in Vancouver and lost 6-4. Since it was the final game before the Christmas break, the team had a little party at the hotel. Quinn arrived at about 11:30 p.m., stayed only about 15 minutes, and left. I just thought he was upset about the loss and didn't feel in a party mood. It was later divulged that Quinn left to meet that night with Canucks officials, and according to a subsequent NHL report, he executed a written contact to become president and general manager of Vancouver. The Canucks were not a good team that year, finishing last in the Smythe Division and drawing small, quiet crowds.

On the Kings' bus to the airport the next morning, not knowing that Quinn had agreed to become an executive with Vancouver I said to him, "Pat, can you imagine watching shitty hockey like that every night?"

He nodded his head and mumbled something, and I didn't realize until weeks later the cutting nature of my remark.

On January 8, 1987, Kings owner Dr. Jerry Buss informed the NHL that Quinn had agreed to join Vancouver at the end of the current season. NHL president John Ziegler Jr. launched a full investigation into the matter, wherein he discovered that, in the Kings' contract with Quinn, the Kings had an option to extend Quinn's contract for one more year by giving Quinn notice to that effect prior to October 1, 1986.

In early December, Vancouver discovered that no "notice of employment" regarding Quinn had been filed with the NHL. Quinn's representative told Vancouver that Quinn was free to discuss employment with Vancouver. On December 9, Vancouver delivered to Quinn a written offer to become president and general manager of the Canucks beginning July 1, 1987. Quinn was to receive $100,000 USD as a signing bonus on or before January 23, 1987.

On December 26, 1986, Quinn told the Kings that he had taken a job with Vancouver but suggested it be kept confidential so he could finish the season as the Kings coach. Kings general manager Rogie Vachon informed Kings owner Dr. Jerry Buss of the situation later that day. Quinn continued to coach the Kings to victories over Boston and Philadelphia on December 27 and 30.

On January 2, 1987, the Kings were in Vancouver for a game that night; at the morning skate, Vancouver's check for $100,000 was delivered to Quinn. Quinn did not inform the Kings about the acceptance of the check.

On January 30, Ziegler handed down his decision. He said, "Although all parties believed they were doing that which was correct, legal, and proper, it is clear that at some point everyone forgot the essential and crucial element of the professional sports business, to wit, the integrity of the competition. By neglecting and failing to remove Quinn as coach from December 26, 1986, to January 9, 1987, Los Angeles permitted a serious threat to the integrity of each game."

He then fined the Kings $10,000 for each day Quinn was not removed as coach for a total of $130,000.

As for Vancouver, Ziegler said, "By its payment of $100,000 in midseason to a coach of a competing team, its closest competitor, it put in jeopardy every game that Quinn would coach for the remainder of the season. In addition, they should have known that, once they had reached their agreement, Quinn could no longer remain coach of Los Angeles. Consequently, for each of the days between December 11, 1986, the date of the agreement in principle and January 9, 1987, Vancouver is fined $10,000 per day for a total of $280,000. In addition for meeting with Quinn while he was still coach of Los Angeles, Vancouver is fined $20,000."

For paying Quinn bonus money to sign, the Canucks were fined an additional $10,000. The total of fines levied on Vancouver was $310,000.

Ziegler also ordered the expulsion of Quinn from the NHL until the Kings and Canucks had completed their regular-season and playoff games. In addition, Quinn was suspended from performing any coaching duties for Vancouver at any time for three years prior to the start of training camp in 1990. Quinn was also suspended from performing any functions or attending league meetings or drafts. He could not conduct any transactions with any other teams, players, draft choices, coaches, assistant coaches, or scouts until after the conclusion of the 1987 annual meeting of the NHL Board of Governors.

One wondered how Quinn, who had a law degree, thought he could continue coaching the Kings while signed with Vancouver. He would have been privy to Kings' plans for players, trades, draft choices, and other affairs, all the while knowing he would be working for their closest competitor.

The Kings then announced that assistant coach Mike Murphy would be head coach for the remainder of the season and that negotiations were underway for a longer contract.

THE 'JAVELIN' INCIDENT

Early in the 1991-92 season, a bizarre incident took place in front of a sold-out crowd 16,005 during a Kings home game. Kings head coach Tom Webster had been bothered by an inner-ear problem that affected his balance. He missed three games with the condition on November 7, 9, and 11. He was back behind the bench on November 12 at Vancouver, but the Kings lost 8-2.

On November 16, the Detroit Red Wings were in Los Angeles, and the incident took place 6:21 into the second period. Kings defenseman Larry Robinson was given a two-minute penalty for cross-checking and a 10-minute penalty for game misconduct. Coach Webster was incensed by the call, so he picked up a hockey stick. As referee Kerry Fraser skated in the vicinity of the Kings bench, Webster, holding the stick javelin-style, let it fly at Fraser.

Luckily, the stick didn't strike the referee, but Webster was ejected from the game, and the Kings lost 5-3.

Webster coached four more games, but on November 27, NHL Executive Vice President Brian O'Neill suspended Webster for 12 games and the team was fined $10,000. The suspension started on November 28 and lasted through December 29. Assistant coaches Cap Raeder and Rick Wilson handled the coaching duties. The Kings went 3-8-1 in that stretch.

Webster returned to coach on December 31 in Vancouver, and the Kings lost 5-3. Two nights later, Webster got his 100th career-coaching victory as the Kings beat Edmonton 5-3 in L.A.

The Kings probably never again used the term, "Let's stick it to 'em."

DON'T COUNT CHICKENS

The old adage, "Don't count your chickens before they're hatched," came true for me in a most embarrassing way at the end of the 2003-04 season.

On March 16, 2004, Coach Andy Murray needed just one more victory—with 11 games remaining—to become the winningest coach in Kings history. The producer of our television-pregame show wanted me to interview Murray before the game that night with the St. Louis Blues. I figured the Kings would beat the Blues, so my final words of the interview were, "Andy, let me be the first to congratulate you on becoming the Kings' winningest coach ever."

Well, not only did the Kings lose that night, they went on to lose 11-straight games to finish the season, a club-record. After each loss, our television producer, Bob Borgen, would point at me on the bus or plane and say, "It's your fault." Never in the world did I think Andy wouldn't get that one victory before the end of the season.

The most bizarre and devastating loss came in the final game of the season at San Jose. The Kings had a 3-1 lead with just over 20 seconds remaining. On television, we had a shot of Murray on the bench, and I was seconds away from saying, "*Now*, Andy Murray will be the winningest coach in Kings history."

Fortunately, I didn't say that because what followed was the most unbelievable ending I've ever seen. The Sharks pulled their goaltender for an extra attacker, and defenseman Brad Stuart scored with 20 seconds left to pull San Jose within a goal at 3-2. Seventeen seconds later, Stuart scored again to tie the game and send it to overtime. Three minutes and ten seconds into overtime, Vincent Damphousse scored to give San Jose the 4-3 win and the Kings their 11th-consecutive loss to end the season.

I'd never seen Murray so despondent. He sat, slumped in his seat, and didn't say a single word on the flight home. When we landed, he bolted off the plane and was about 100 yards ahead of everyone as he walked to his car.

The following year, 2004-05, was the NHL lockout, canceling the season; so Murray didn't get another chance until the first game of the 2005-06 season in Dallas. The Kings jumped out to a 4-0 lead at the end of the first period. Again, it looked as if Murray would attain that elusive record-breaking win, but Dallas came back with five straight goals and won 5-4.

Finally, the next night—October 6, 2005—the Kings beat the Phoenix Coyotes 3-2 in front of a sold-out crowd of 18,118 in the home opener, and Andy Murray had win No. 179, passing Bob Pulford as the Kings' all-time winningest coach.

I'd learned my lesson, though—never predict while announcing sports.

THE COBRA

From 1976 to 1978, the Kings had a backup goaltender named Gary "Cobra" Simmons. The nickname came from the picture of a green cobra snake on the front of his black goalie mask. He didn't play very often, but on March 9, 1978, Cobra got the call to mind the net on the road against the Buffalo Sabres. It was his first start in 20 games—and he was a little rusty. The Sabres scored the first two goals.

"I was so slow on one of them I even missed it coming *out* of the net," Cobra said.

The Kings rallied, and the game ended 3-3. Afterward, a reporter asked Cobra, who had just played his first game in 48 days, if he thought he would start the next game.

"What do you think I am?" Cobra answered. "A f—ing machine?'

TRIPLE-CROWN LINE

On January 13, 1979, Kings head coach Bob Berry made a monumental decision. Hockey coaches are always tinkering with line combinations—whom to play together on the wings with a certain center, always looking for that chemistry that will make the line click. That night, with the Kings playing in Detroit, Berry decided to put left wing Charlie Simmer and right wing Dave Taylor together with center Marcel Dionne. That was the start of one of the highest scoring lines in NHL history.

The Kings beat Detroit that night 7-3, and that line came to be known as the Triple-Crown Line. The next full season they were together, they compiled 328 points, the second most in one season of any line in league history. Dionne finished that season with 137 points and the NHL scoring title. Simmer shared the league lead with 56 goals and set a modern-day NHL record by scoring a goal in 13 consecutive games, and Taylor, despite missing 19 games with a knee injury, still managed to score 90 points. From January 13, 1979, to November 17, 1979, that line scored at least a point in 56 straight games.

Each player was a perfect complement for the others, and they had that sixth sense of where each would be on the ice at any given moment. Dave Taylor was the banger in the corners, and he would get control of the puck. Dionne was what they call a pure goal scorer—one who had that special knack for putting the puck in the net. Simmer, while also a great goal scorer, tallied most of his from close range of the net and was also adept at having the puck glance off his body for a score.

The most devastating night that line experienced was on March 2, 1981, at Maple Leaf Gardens in Toronto. Simmer had scored 56 goals in 65 games and was the team's leading goal scorer as the Kings met the Maple Leafs. At one point in the game, Simmer was chasing one of the Toronto players and went to turn to go after the puck. Toronto defenseman Borje Salming just nicked his shoulder, but spun him around. As Simmer put it, "I skated around my foot."

In other words, one foot stayed anchored while his body twisted around it and caused a spiral fracture of his right leg.

In the booth, I could tell it seemed to be a severe injury, but my first indication of how serious was when Marcel Dionne skated over to Simmer, took one look at his leg, and started shaking his head. In my earphone, our producer in the remote truck was telling me it was a broken leg. I wanted to know who was giving him that information and how accurate it was before I mentioned that on the air.

The trainers took Simmer into the Toronto dressing room because it was the closest to the area where the injury had occurred.

"What do you think?" the doctor asked Charlie.

"I broke my leg," Charlie replied.

"How do you know?" the doctor inquired.

"I broke my f—-ing leg!" he hollered back again.

They taped both of his legs together, and when the ambulance attendants dropped the stretcher off the curb and headed to the ambulance, Charlie said it started to hurt.

When they arrived at the hospital, shock started to set in. The nurses said to Simmer, "We were watching the game on television, and we knew you were coming here." Simmer had surgery the next morning, and his season was finished.

Looking back on the injury, Simmer said, "If you're going to break your leg, you want to do it on a Saturday night with the game being televised coast to coast on *Hockey Night in Canada*. That way everyone can see it. You don't want to do it on a Thursday night in Pittsburgh."

Eight days later on March 10, 1981, the Kings traded their first-round choice in the 1983 draft and their third-round choice in the 1981 draft to the Buffalo Sabres for high-scoring winger Rick Martin to compensate for the offensive loss of Simmer. Martin had twice scored more than 50 goals a season. The trade turned out to be a disaster. Martin had a knee injury, but doctors in Buffalo and in Los Angeles assured Kings general manager George Maguire that Martin could play. One morning shortly after the trade, Maguire asked me to go to the L.A. airport and pick up Martin. As I waited at the curb, I could see Martin walking toward me almost dragging one leg. I introduced myself and told him I would drive him to the Forum. As he got in my car, he had to lift his leg with two hands just to bend his knee. I thought, "We traded a No.1 draft choice for this?"

As it turned out, Rick Martin played only four games for the Kings, scoring two goals and four assists for six points. One night, shortly thereafter prior to a game at the Forum, the Kings called a press conference to announce that Martin's knees were so bad he would have to retire. A reporter for KABC radio, the late Liz Shanov, asked the Kings' George Maguire if Scotty Bowman, then-general manager at Buffalo, had screwed him on the deal.

George replied, "Scotty Bowman couldn't screw anybody, including you."

By the way, with the No. 1 draft choice that Buffalo received from the Kings in the 1983 draft, the Sabres chose Tom Barrasso, who went on to become one of the most dominant goaltenders in the NHL.

DIONNE DEATH THREAT

Marcel Dionne played 12 years for the Kings and remains the team's all-time leading scorer. He was the first true superstar to wear a Kings uniform, and he was a favorite among Kings fans who marveled at this scoring ability; but apparently that appreciation was not shared in other arenas around the NHL.

On January 27, 1979, the Kings were playing in Pittsburgh, and Dionne received a phone call that afternoon at the team hotel. The caller said, "I have a high-powered rifle; and if you score a goal tonight, I'm going to blow your head off."

Dionne told Coach Bob Berry, who told him not to tell anyone else on the team, and then he reported the threat to security. Security told Dionne they thought it was a hoax, but he didn't have to play if he didn't feel safe. Marcel said he was going to play, and the NHL provided security for him as he entered and exited the ice. On the ice, however, he was on his own.

Dionne was not known to exert himself too much during the pregame warm-up. He would usually skate leisurely around the ice, but on that night during the warm-up he was skating fast and zigzagging all over the ice, feeling that it would be hard to hit a moving target. His teammates, not knowing the situation, wondered what had gotten into Marcel. During the national anthem, Marcel felt he was a "sitting duck" on the bench, so he kept rocking from side to side.

When the game started, linemates Dave Taylor and Charlie Simmer kept passing the puck to Dionne, but Marcel wanted no part of it so he kept passing it back. He even passed up a couple of great scoring opportunities, thinking he would be shot if he scored. Finally, he had the puck with a wide-open net and couldn't do anything but score.

After the puck went in, Marcel said, "I looked for the biggest guys on the ice and skated into the middle of them trying to hide."

Dionne scored two goals that night, the Kings won 5-3, and fortunately, the call was a hoax.

The next day, word of the death threat got out; and the next time the Kings played in Pittsburgh, security screened all the team's phone calls. Marcel said he had put the threat out of his mind, but his teammates apparently thought the person who made the threat might be in the crowd. In hockey, the custom is, when a player scores a goal, his teammates on the ice skate over to congratulate him. That night, when Marcel scored, all of his teammates scattered in all different directions, just in case. Charlie Simmer said, "When a teammate scores a goal. and you return to the bench, you want to sit close to him because you know the television cameras will be focused on him. But not that night—we all gave Marcel plenty of room on the bench."

Marcel said when he tells that story now at various functions, he says, "We never played as a team because nobody wanted to die as a team."

CAN YOU SAY THAT ON TV?

One never knows how players are going to react or what they will say on live television.

Dave "Tiger" Williams played for the Kings from 1984 to 1988 appearing in 162 games scoring 40 goals and 50 assists for 90 points, but he was best known for his volatile play on the ice and for amassing 962 penalty minutes in a Kings uniform. That total pales in comparison to his final career total of 3,966 penalty minutes, which is a NHL record. On describing himself as a player he responded, "Never surrender—I wanted everybody to be like me. If they didn't put their life on the line, I wouldn't like them, their wife, or their family."

Tiger was known for saying things without regard to the consequences. One time, while boarding a commercial flight in Los Angeles, Tiger spotted a passenger we didn't know smoking a cigarette in *Tiger's* seat. Tiger pounced. "You stupid bastard, don't you know you're not supposed to smoke while the plane is at the gate?" The startled passenger quickly extinguished his cigarette. Another time on a commercial flight, Tiger was putting his luggage in the overhead bin when he spotted a woman coming down the aisle wearing the ugliest hat of all time. As she passed Tiger, he said, "Lady, don't tell me you paid for that hat."

On December 5, 1985, the Kings were playing in Edmonton and were losing 4-0 early in the second period. They then scored four straight on goals by Dave Taylor, Brian MacLellan, Garry Galley, and Phil Sykes to tie the score. In the third period, Williams scored with 2:58 left in the game and the Kings led 6-5. However, with 41 seconds remaining, the Oilers tied the score, and the game ended 6-6 in overtime.

On a live postgame TV interview, my partner Nick Nickson said to Williams, "Tiger, I thought you had scored the game winning goal."

Tiger responded, "Mr. Nickson, it should have been the game-winning goal, but each time this team gets close to winning we just …" and with this Tiger grabbed his throat with both hands and started choking himself, "… aaarrrggghhh."

Nickson then mentioned that the Oilers had outshot the Kings 46 to 26 in the game, and Tiger said, "Yes, but a lot of those were wimp-ass shots."

We didn't do too many more live interviews with Tiger.

***

Another incident involving Tiger Williams occurred at the Kings practice facility, the Culver City Ice Rink. The Kings dressing room was located upstairs on the second floor and was a long and narrow room. The players' lockers were across from each other so that when they were sitting and bent over tying their skates, there wasn't much more than a narrow pathway down the middle. As the players arrived for practice this particular day, Bernie Nicholls noticed two boxes filled with copies of a new book written by Tiger Williams. The books had been delivered to Tiger at the practice rink. Tiger had not arrived in the room so, as a joke, Nicholls passed out the book saying they were a gift from Tiger. Tiger had no intention of "giving" the books away; he was going to sell them.

Tiger had been in the medical room talking with trainer Pete Demers and a friend who was showing him a high-tech bow and arrow. Tiger was known for hunting bear with bow and arrow in the off-season. When Tiger got to the locker room, some of the players, including Nicholls, were mockingly thanking him for the gift. Tiger was so incensed he took the bow and arrow, hollered at Nicholls, and fired an arrow about eight inches into a metal air duct at the end of the room. If one player had leaned the wrong way, or someone had gotten up and walked into the middle of the room at the instant Tiger fired, the outcome would have been disastrous.

***

Another player's reaction on a live postgame interview took us by surprise. It was on January 21, 1985, again in Edmonton. The Kings led 4-0 in the first period on goals by Brian MacLellan, Bob Miller (not me), Marcel Dionne, and Carl Mokosak. Dionne's goal was the 611th of his career to move him past Bobby Hull into third place all time on the NHL goal-scoring list. By the end of the second period, the Kings led 7-3 and were well on their way to a victory over a strong Edmonton team, or so we thought. The Oilers scored five goals in the third period to win 8-7.

Nickson's live guest on the TV postgame show that night was Kings right-winger Jim Fox. Fox was so distraught and upset over the way the Kings blew the game that he was actually in tears. When Nick asked what went wrong he said, "Who cares? It happened. ... We're awful." Fox later said he was frustrated and at a loss for words, and he felt ashamed that he actually cried on live television. I told him I thought it was one of the greatest reactions I had ever seen because it showed everyone his true emotions and the true competitive nature of the sport, i.e., how much they want to win.

I thought it was a great moment of live television.

FOXED OUT OF A GOAL

On the Kings' all-time scoring list, my broadcast partner, Jim Fox, is credited with 186 goals in his NHL career, but it should be 187.

On February 1, 1987, the Kings were playing the Quebec Nordiques in Quebec City when Fox ripped a shot into the net. The puck went in, hit the metal bar in the back of the net, and came out so fast that play continued as the Nordiques headed down the ice with the puck. Fox, meanwhile, stayed in front of the Quebec net, slamming his stick on the ice, jumping up and down, and screaming that he had scored. He didn't attempt to join the play at the other end. On our telecast, I said that Fox had scored, but then I had my doubts as play continued. At a break in the action, we showed a replay, and sure enough, the puck went right into the middle of the net. In those days, there was no television replay for officials to check.

By coincidence, the referee in that game, Andy Van Helle-mond, had asked the Kings before the game if he could ride on their charter flight to Toronto that night. The Kings agreed. On the bus to the airport, Van Hellemond was sitting in an aisle seat next to me when Fox boarded, stopped in the aisle, and stared at Van Hellemond. The referee said, "Jim, I'm sorry, I didn't see it go in the net, nor did either of the linesmen. I can't call a goal if I didn't see it."

Van Hellemond told me the officials looked at a television replay between periods and knew the goal should have counted. He also said to the linesmen, "Watch, this will end up a one-goal game."

Sure enough, it ended Quebec 3 - Kings 2.

KELLY VERSUS HOWE

Gordie Howe had a remarkable career in hockey playing for 26 seasons in the NHL, 25 of those with the Detroit Red Wings and one with the Hartford Whalers. In addition, he played six seasons in the World Hockey Association, playing with two of his sons. He retired when he was 52 years old after playing 2,186 total games.

On December 12, 1979, Howe had a rude awakening while playing for the Whalers against the Kings in Los Angeles. Unfortunately, only 8,732 fans were on hand to see one of the greatest players in the history of the game, although he was at the end of his career.

The Kings had a muscular young rookie named John Paul Kelly, and he made a name for himself on that night. As Howe brought the puck to center ice, Kelly threw a body check and knocked Howe completely over the boards into the penalty box. The crowd gasped as they saw Howe tumble out of sight. Kelly said later, "I thought, 'Oh, my God … I've checked a 52-year-old grandfather, the legendary Gordie Howe, over the boards.'"

Howe said later he thought there was Plexiglas in front of the penalty box, and he would just take the check and bounce off the glass, but there was no glass at that point.

Howe was known throughout his career for having the "sharpest elbows in hockey" and he wasn't shy about using them to inflict bodily harm on opponents. Players on the bench told coach Bob Berry that he'd better get J.P. off the ice before Howe went at him. Nothing further occurred between Howe and Kelly, but it was a sight to remember.

VACHON GOAL

On February 15, 1977, hockey fans at the L.A. Forum thought they had been in on hockey history. This was the 59th year of the NHL and the 14,280th game; up to that time, no goalie had ever been credited with scoring a goal.

With the Kings leading the New York Islanders 1-0 in the first period, a delayed penalty was called against the Kings' Bert Wilson. The Islanders, in possession of the puck, pulled goalie Glenn "Chico" Resch for an extra attacker, and teammate Bryan Trottier passed the puck from deep in the Kings' zone to his defensemen at the Kings' blue line. The puck went between the defensemen, however, and slid 188 feet into an empty net for a Kings goal.

The official scorer thought that Kings goalie Rogie Vachon had been the last King to touch the puck before the Islanders gained possession and that he should get credit for the goal. The 10,256 fans in attendance roared when Vachon's name was announced as the goal scorer. After the period, while listening to an audio tape of my play-by-play, I realized that, after Vachon had made a save, I had said that the Kings' Vic Venasky played the puck, so it couldn't have been Vachon's goal. I mentioned this to the scorer, and after some discussion, the goal was changed to Venasky.

Sorry Rogie!

Vachon did get the shutout in a 3-0 win.

For your information, Billy Smith, who was the Islanders' backup goalie that night, became the first goalie to get credit for a goal on November 28, 1979, against the Colorado Rockies.

ESA "PENIS"

One of the biggest changes and challenges over the past several years has been the influx of European players in the NHL and the effort it takes to pronounce their names correctly. In the 2003-04 season the Kings had a newcomer to the team, a forward from Finland named Esa Pirnes, pronounced PEER-nes. The potential for trouble concerning his last name never entered my mind, but disaster struck as the Kings were playing the Phoenix Coyotes one night at Staples Center.

The battle for the puck was along the boards when, on the air, I said, "Here is Esa Peni … er, Pirnes." I didn't quite say the "s" in penis, but it sounded like it. I paused and then heard my partner Jim Fox on the talkback to the control room shouting, "Did he say it? Did he say it?" I couldn't speak for a few seconds, and the next time I looked toward Jim, his chair was empty. He was in the back of the booth, laughing so hard he was crying.

After the game, Kings coach Andy Murray played a tape of that incident for the entire team. The next morning, we were leaving on a road trip, and as I was walking toward the plane, Pirnes was walking toward me shaking his head. He told me that when he returned home that game, he had four messages on his voicemail from friends in Finland, saying, "Did that guy call you 'Penis?'"

We both had a good laugh and so did Esa's teammates. I told most other announcers in the NHL what had happened hoping I wouldn't be the only one to make that mistake. The next telecast, the first time Pirnes touched the puck, I said, "Here comes Esa Peeeer-nes to center ice." I still had to pause a bit before saying his name to make sure I enunciated correctly.

FINAL INTERMISSION

GRETZKY TO L.A.

Bruce McNall purchased 100 percent of the Kings team from Jerry Buss on March 23, 1988, and the rotund, jovial new owner made an immediate impact.

In the summer of 1988, there were rumors that the Kings were trying to acquire the greatest player in the game, Wayne Gretzky of the Edmonton Oilers. I thought it was too good to be true, but I wanted to find out for myself if the rumors had any validity. I phoned McNall under the pretense of talking about the television schedule for the coming season, and toward the end of the conversation, I went for it, saying, "When are you going to sign Gretzky?"

There was a lengthy pause and then Bruce said, "Tell me what you think of this: we unveil new silver-and-black uniforms, and Wayne Gretzky is our model."

I said it would be fantastic, so I knew a deal was in the works.

In early August, I was at the Forum when Jerry West, general manager of the Los Angeles Lakers, whispered to me, "The deal is done." He said he had played golf with someone who told him that Gretzky was coming to the Kings.

Sure enough, the next day I got a call to be the master of ceremonies at the press conference that night at a Los Angeles hotel. The media response was unbelievable, with about 12 television stations, some going live on the air, and about 30 still photographers. At the dais, McNall made some introductions then said, with tongue in cheek, "... But now, the reason we're here, and the moment you've been waiting for, the introduction of our new team colors and uniforms."

He then paused for reaction then continued, "May we have our model please?"

Out stepped Wayne and Janet Gretzky. When Wayne put on his Kings jersey, the sound of the still cameras clicking was like machine-gun fire. As Gretzky was facing the audience, someone yelled in jest, "What number did you get?" as if he would get anything other than his famous No. 99

This was the biggest trade in sports history. At no other time had an athlete in his prime, one who dominated his sport the way Wayne Gretzky did, been traded.

Many people said it was like Babe Ruth being traded, but I disagree. When Ruth was traded from Boston to the New York Yankees, he wasn't the Ruth who later in his career dominated the game. This trade was headlines around the world. I had a friend who told me he was vacationing in Germany, and it made headlines in the papers there.

The reaction in Los Angeles was immediate. The Kings rose from near obscurity to one of the highest-profile teams in the United States and Canada. *Playboy* magazine called Gretzky, "Jim Thorpe on skates, Jesse Owens with a stick, and Babe Ruth in hockey pants. On statistics alone, Gretzky is the greatest athlete of the 20th Century."

The Kings had to get extra help to man the phones in the ticket office to serve thousands calling to purchase season tickets. When told they weren't sure of the price of tickets, fans often said, "Here's my credit card, just fill it in later." The Kings sold something like 4,000 season tickets in a week, and their season-ticket base rose from 5,000 to 9,000. Kings merchandise—jersey, jackets, and caps—went from last in the NHL to the No. 1-selling item and were in great demand throughout the U.S. and Canada, not just in L.A. In fact, while on vacation in Europe, I saw someone wearing a Kings T-shirt in Rothenburg, Germany, and a street sweeper wearing a Kings hat in Salzburg, Austria. The trade also had an impact on the Kings television schedule, which was increased from 37 to 62 games.

Reaction around the NHL included Emile Francis, general manager of the Hartford Whalers saying, "The Kings went from the outhouse to the penthouse in one fell swoop." The Kings were now the "in" team in Hollywood. McNall had a "Meet the Kings" party at famous Chasen's restaurant in Beverly Hills. In attendance were Milton Berle, Michael J. Fox, John Candy, Neil Diamond, Mary Hart, Alan Thicke, and Jamie Farr. Season-ticket holders included Magic Johnson, Rob Lowe, and Tom Hanks. Former president Ronald Reagan and wife, Nancy, watched many games from ice level at the glass.

Some loyal Kings fans had a different reaction however. Gretzky was not a favorite of Kings fans when he played for Edmonton. One night in a game at the Forum, the Kings' Dave Taylor took a swing at Gretzky and just grazed him, but Gretzky fell to the ice as if he'd been shot. Wayne was peeking up at the referee to see if a penalty was being called. It was, and then Gretzky jumped up and continued playing as the crowd lustily booed. Kings fans would wave white handkerchiefs at Gretzky because he was always "crying" over missed calls by the referee. When Gretzky came to the Kings, those same fans came to games wearing buttons that read, "I was a Kings fan BG," *Before Gretzky*. They almost seemed to resent the fact that so many new fans jumped on the Kings bandwagon.

The first game for Wayne in a Kings uniform was October 6, 1988, and a sellout crowd packed the building and roared their approval as Gretzky was introduced. In typical Gretzky fashion, he scored on his first shot on goal at 12:54 of the first period and finished with a goal and three assists in a 8-2 Kings win over Detroit.

I have told people that those of us who were able to see Wayne Gretzky night after night were fortunate. I always approached our telecast each night as if I might see and be able to describe something that I'd never seen before. I feel, years from now, fans are going to ask us what it was like watching him play in person, much as you would ask someone who saw Babe Ruth in his prime.

6

OVERTIME

GRETZKY RECORDS

October 15, 1989, will go down in National Hockey League history as a most significant date. That's the night Wayne Gretzky became the greatest scorer in the history of the game. He passed the legendary Gordie Howe with his 1,851st point, and he did it in true Gretzky fashion.

First let's go back to the summer of 1989. It was obvious that Gretzky would break Howe's record early in the coming season. One day, a friend of mine asked me what I was going to say when it happened. I told him I was just going to do the play-by-play and hope I didn't make a mistake because I would hear it the rest of my life. But then, he said, "Aren't you going to say something special?"

I hadn't thought about that, but then I thought people apparently expect something more than just the description of the play. I started jotting down some ideas, but I didn't want it to sound rehearsed. The night of the game, I told our television producer, Mark Stulberger, to give me about six seconds to say something after it happened; and then I would be quiet, and he could get crowd noise and reaction shots.

The moment came, of all places, in Edmonton, where Gretzky had so many great moments playing for the Oilers. At the start of the game, I asked my partner, Nick Nickson, to help me out and point to the ice when Gretzky was playing and away from the ice when he was on the bench. That may sound stupid, but I didn't want Gretzky to jump on the ice, "on the fly," when I'd be unaware of his presence. As it turned out, fans watching on television and listening on radio appreciated that since, when I said Gretzky is on the ice, they would be on the edge of their chairs; and when I said he was on the bench, they would relax. They didn't know I was doing it more for myself than for their benefit.

The historic moment came with just 53 seconds remaining in regulation. The Oilers, leading 4-3, won a face-off in their zone. Oilers defenseman Kevin Lowe cleared the puck high in the air, but Kings defenseman Steve Duchesne knocked it down at the blue line and passed to Dave Taylor, who slid the puck to his left to Gretzky—who then backhanded it past Oilers goalie Bill Ranford. As the Kings players streamed onto the ice, I said, "Wayne Gretzky, the Great One, has become the greatest of them all—the leading scorer in the history of the National Hockey League."

Nothing profound, but at least it put a capper on the moment.

Some events in Gretzky's career seem to be right out of a Hollywood script, and this was one of those moments. Play was stopped for an on-ice ceremony featuring Gordie Howe; Wayne; his wife, Janet; his father, Walter; Kings owner Bruce McNall; Scotty Morrison from the Hockey Hall of Fame; and NHL President John Ziegler, Jr. In his remarks Gretzky said, "Maybe it is only fitting that a reward such as this takes a lot of teamwork and a lot of help; and both teams here today are definitely a big part of the 1,800 points I've gotten in my career."

There was still a game to finish, and it went into overtime, where the Kings won 5-4 on a wrap-around goal by—you guessed it—Wayne Gretzky.

To give you an idea of how great Gretzky was, it took Howe 26 seasons to reach 1,850 points, and Gretzky broke the record just six games into his 12th season. Four seasons later, Gretzky was set to break another of Howe's records, the one for *goals* scored in the NHL. This time it came in front of a home crowd at the Forum on March 23, 1994. The sell-out crowd of 16,005 anticipated this would be the night that they'd witness hockey history. There were over 100 requests for press credentials for that game. Again I thought, "I've got to come up with something special to say after he scores."

The historic moment came at 14:47 of the second period against the Vancouver Canucks. Luc Robitaille passed to Gretzky, who then passed to Marty McSorley on the right side. As Vancouver goalie Kirk McLean came out to play a possible shot by McSorley, Marty slid the puck across the ice to his left to Gretzky, who was wide open, along with the net. As he scored, I said on television, "Wayne Gretzky's NHL record book is now complete. He's the all-time leader in points, assists, and now, with his 802nd goal, the all-time leading goal scorer in the history of the National Hockey League."

Gretzky broke the record in 650 games fewer than Howe took to reach 801.

Again, the game was stopped for an on-ice ceremony, which included Wayne's wife, Janet; his mother and father, Phyllis and Walter; and NHL Commissioner Gary Bettman. In Wayne's speech, he said, "To the fans of L.A., I've loved playing here for six years, and I hope I get another six years."

But that was not to happen.

GRETZKY TO ST. LOUIS

After eight years with the Kings, the unbelievable happened: the Kings traded Gretzky to St. Louis on February 27, 1996, for Craig Johnson, Patrice Tardif, Roman Vopat, and first- and fifth-round draft choices.

In January of that season, Gretzky delivered what some termed "an ultimatum" to the Kings: "Get some talent through immediate trades or trade me. I need to see action now. This city deserves to be winners. I'd like to win, and I'd like to see that happen."

He felt the Kings were two players away from contending for a Stanley Cup, and he was frustrated over management's inability to pull off a trade. He wanted them to acquire a 50-goal scorer and an offensive-minded defenseman. Gretzky would have become an unrestricted free agent that coming summer. In that situation, he would have been free to sign with any other team without the Kings receiving any compensation. "For me," said Gretzky, "I would like to have the opportunity to win a championship."

Gretzky's agent, Michael Barnett, held a meeting with Kings management on January 16 and said, "Ideally, a resolution will see him retire as a King and end all the rumors. No demand for a trade to another team was discussed today. It's not even in Wayne's thoughts at this time."

Sam McMaster, the Kings general manager, said of the meeting that day, "We discussed many things, including a contract extension for Wayne. Our goal is to build a winner and keep Wayne Gretzky as part of that organization."

On February 27, McMaster said the Kings offered Gretzky a two-year contract extension. On television that night, Gretzky told KCAL-TV that, as a result of that afternoon's meeting, the Kings left the decision to him, saying, "Do you want to sign with us, or do you want us to trade you?"

Gretzky went home, discussed the situation with his wife; and in a news conference at 8 p.m., the Kings announced they had traded Gretzky to St. Louis. Bob Sanderman, representing Kings owner Philip Anschutz and Ed Roski Jr., said, "Wayne let us know this afternoon that he preferred not to remain a Los Angeles King during his remaining active [playing] days." The Kings said they had also offered Wayne a "senior" position with the club when his playing days were over. They said he was the one who chose to leave.

Regardless, the Kings were roundly criticized in the media. Helene Elliott, of the *Los Angeles Times*, wrote, "Goodbye to the best player to ever wear a Kings uniform—or any other in hockey—and goodbye to all hopes of seeing the Kings rise above the mediocrity they have so tightly embraced for so many years."

Michael Ventre, in the *L.A. Daily News* was more blunt, "Trading Wayne Gretzky to the St. Louis Blues ranks as the all-time imbecilic act in the history of the Kings franchise."

So, the most exciting era in Kings hockey had ended.

During Gretzky's stay in L.A., there were reports—which he denied—that he had a hand in trades made by the team. This feeling was perpetuated, in my opinion, when on team flights after games, Wayne would sit next to owner McNall. I'm sure some players who may have struggled in the game that night felt that Wayne was telling Bruce they should be traded. Wayne admitted that there were times when the Kings were contemplating a trade and they would ask his opinion of certain players whom they might acquire, especially if he had played with those players. Certainly, that was a prudent thing to do—ask the opinion of as great a player as Gretzky. Another problem was, at times, McNall would invite several players to fly with him on his private jet to the next game rather than take the team plane. Those players included many of Gretzky's former Oilers teammates who were current members of the Kings; and there seemed to be some resentment among other players who called the exclusive group, "The Magnificent Seven."

7

PLAYOFFS

MIRACLE ON MANCHESTER

The greatest single game I have ever witnessed or been a part of was a 1982 playoff game between the Kings and the Edmonton Oilers. It's known as the "Miracle on Manchester," named for the street that runs by the Forum—then the Home of the Kings.

The best-of-five playoff series started in Edmonton, and the Oilers were heavily favored since they had finished the regular season with 111 points, second overall in the NHL. The Kings finished with 63 points, 17th overall. That was the lowest Kings point total in 10 years. The Oilers also boasted of a potent line-up that included Wayne Gretzky, who had scored a NHL-record 92 goals that season, Paul Coffey, Mark Messier, Jari Kurri, Kevin Lowe, and Grant Fuhr.

The first game of the series was played in Edmonton on April 7, 1982, and no one gave the Kings any chance for an upset. Playoff games are usually tight-checking, low-scoring affairs; but this night the Kings and Oilers set a NHL record for most goals by both teams with a total of 18 as the Kings won 10-8. The Oilers led 4-1 in the first period, but the Kings came back and led 8-6 at the end of the second. With the game tied 8-8 in the third period, Charlie Simmer scored as the puck bounced off his leg for a 9-8 Kings lead. Kings goalie Mario Lessard then stopped Gretzky on a breakaway, and Bernie Nicholls scored for the Kings into an empty net for the 10-8 victory.

The Oilers of that season were extremely arrogant, and that arrogance extended throughout the entire organization. They had a scout named Bob Freeman who sat in the booth right next to our broadcast location. The walls of the booth did not extend all the way out, so a person sitting in the next booth could hear what we were saying. At one point in the game, Gretzky was complaining to the referees about a call, and I said on the air, "Well, Wayne Gretzky is crying again to the officials."

Freeman overheard this and yelled at me, "Why don't you shut up? You don't know what you're talking about!" So when Nicholls scored into the empty net to secure the win, I really went overboard in my call of the goal just to irk Freeman. Nicholls had a celebration he did after scoring a goal that consisted of skating bent over, and pumping his arms back and forth. It became known as the "Pumpernicholl." When he scored into the empty net, I shouted, in an uncharacteristic display of *homerism*, "Do the 'Pumpernicholl,' Bernie. Yeah!"

The Oilers won the next game 3-2 in overtime on a goal by Gretzky, and the teams headed for Los Angeles with the series tied one game apiece. The scene was set for "The Miracle on Manchester."

It was April 10, 1982, and a full house of 16,005 filled the Forum in great anticipation of the Kings upsetting the Oilers. Their hopes were quickly dashed. Edmonton jumped out to a 5-0 lead at the end of two periods, and Gretzky was really putting on a show with two goals and two assists. The crowd turned on Gretzky vocally, shouting obscenities at him—they booed him, and they waved white handkerchiefs at him because of his complaining about every referee's call that went against the Oilers. Oilers coach Glen Sather, who always had a smug smirk on his face, said of the Kings crowd, "The people here have the least amount of class in North America." Gretzky said the crowd didn't bother him.

The Oilers were completely outplaying and embarrassing the Kings. In fact, the Oilers were so arrogant that they were actually laughing at the Kings during play. I was so upset because I thought, "We do this every time: get everyone in L.A. excited about hockey and the Kings and then go right in the dumper." No one was prepared, however, for what would occur in the third period.

At 2:46 into that final period, Kings defenseman Jay Wells scored form the left point, and I thought, "At least we weren't going to get shut out." About three minutes later, Kings rookie Doug Smith, standing right in front of the net, put a shot up under the crossbar, and it was 5-2. The next goal didn't come until 5:22 remaining, when Charlie Simmer came from behind the net and jammed the puck past the right goal post to make it 5-3. At that point, the crowd was going crazy, and you could sense a feeling that maybe, just maybe, the Kings could come all the way back.

Kings owner Dr. Jerry Buss sat in a specially constructed private box, which consisted of four seats, at ice level right between the two benches. I noticed the box was empty, and I wondered on the air if the owner had left the game. I found out later Buss had a date with Kathy Crosby, and they had left to head for Palm Springs in a limousine. As the story goes, as they were listening to the game, the chauffeur turned and asked, "Should we go back?" to which Buss said, "No, it seems the farther away we get, the better they play." So the Kings owner missed the greatest comeback in Kings history.

With the Kings trailing 5-3, defenseman Mark Hardy scored on a weak shot from the top of the slot, which fooled Oilers goalie Grant Fuhr. With 4:01 left, it was 5-4. Now there was bedlam in the Forum. With 5:00 left, the Oilers Garry Unger had taken a five-minute major penalty for high sticking and cutting the Kings captain, Dave Lewis, on his eyebrow. Lewis got a two-minute minor for hooking, so the Kings eventually had a three-minute major power play. Still, the Oilers had chances to sew up the game. With 1:37 left, Kings goalie Mario Lessard stopped Edmonton's Pat Hughes on a breakaway. Then with 10 seconds left and the puck in the Oilers zone, Kings right wing Jim Fox made a great play—one that gave the Kings a chance. Gretzky had the puck on his stick, and all he had to do was clear it to center ice so time would run out. Fox, however, skated in front of Gretzky, took the puck away, and passed it to Hardy, who shot from the top of the slot. Fuhr made the save, but the rebound went right in front of the net to Kings rookie Steve Bozek, who scored to tie the game at 5-5.

When I looked at the scoreboard clock, it read 0:05 left.

During the wild finish, Lewis was getting stitched up in the Kings locker room. He said that, when Bozek scored, the doctor, in mid-stitch with needle in hand, pumped his arms in the air, scaring the hell out of Lewis. Meanwhile, in the arena, the crowd was frenzied, screaming, jumping up and down, and roaring. Yet they had 15 minutes to wait for the sudden-death overtime to start.

About a minute into overtime, my heart, and the hearts of 16,000 fans, sank as Lessard came sliding out of the Kings goal, giving Mark Messier a wide-open net. However, Messier shot it wide on his backhand. The Kings were still alive. Two-and-a-half minutes into overtime, there was a face-off in the Oilers zone to the left of goalie Grant Fuhr. The Kings had three rookies out on the forward line: Bozek, Smith, and Daryl Evans. Smith won the draw to Evans, who was positioned on right wing along the boards. Evans shot a one-timer right off the pass—a laser of a shot that went into the net over Fuhr's right shoulder.

The crowd erupted. Evans pirouetted the full length of the ice, twisting and turning, his stick in the air as his teammates leaped off the bench to chase him down and pile on him at the opposite end. The Kings had completed the greatest single-game comeback in NHL Stanley Cup playoff history with a 6-5 win.

Outside the Forum, a wild celebration was taking place in the parking lot. Fans were honking car horns and forming impromptu motorcades in the streets. Some had taken Oilers jerseys, tied them to their car bumpers, and were dragging them along. However, the series wasn't over yet. The Oilers won the next game in L.A. 3-2, and with the series tied two games apiece, the teams head back to Edmonton for the deciding game the *next* night.

After the Kings win in the "miracle" game, Scott Carmichael, the Kings public relations director, had been cheering in the hallway near the dressing rooms. When the Oilers won the next game, Edmonton coach Glen Sather said to Carmichael, "You aren't cheering tonight, are you?" and then swore at him. A minor altercation ensued with Sather taking a swing and grabbing Carmichael's tie. Then some of the Oilers players intervened on behalf of Sather. A local sports reporter, Joe McDonnell, who was extremely heavy, then grabbed Sather from behind. Sather later said he got bear-hugged by a guy who outweighed him by 600 pounds.

Since only one charter plane could be found, both teams flew to Edmonton on the same plane, which was extremely rare. I had never heard of it happening before, and an insurance waiver had to be obtained. The Oilers boarded first and sat in the back, and the Kings sat in front. By the time the plane took off from L.A., it was already 1:30 in the morning in Edmonton, and the game was *that* night.

I remember landing in Edmonton in fog so thick that you literally couldn't see the wing. The plane slammed down on the runway so hard that a bolt broke off in a panel above my head. When the Kings filed into their hotel lobby that morning, a little, elderly cleaning woman was shaking her fist at them saying, "You didn't treat my boys very well in Los Angeles." Mark Hardy looked at her and said, "Lady, it's 5:30 in the morning—go home and go to bed."

The deciding game was played April 13, 1982, and the Kings jumped to a 2-0 lead in the first period on goals by Simmer. Evans then got his fifth goal of the series, and the Kings led 3-2 at the end of the first period. In the second, the Kings got goals from Marcel Dionne, Nicholls, and Dan Bonar, and led 6-2 at the end of two. Bonar scored again in the third, and the Kings won 7-4 to eliminate the heavily favored Oilers.

I was so excited I wanted to call home, but the only pay phone I could find was located near the Oilers dressing room. The Oilers wives and girlfriends were in tears as I shouted to my wife over the phone, "Wasn't that a great game?"

TORONTO '75

The greatest regular season in Kings history was 1974-75, but it had a disappointing end in the playoffs. That season the Kings had the highest point total in team history, 105, lost only 17 games all season, and finished second to Montreal in the Norris Division.

The Norris Division was a strange makeup of Montreal, Pittsburgh, Washington, Detroit, and Los Angeles. It was as if the NHL made up the various divisions and said, "Whom did we leave out? Oh, yes ... L.A." The teams played each other six times—three home and three away—so the Kings logged a lot of road miles and yet had their best season. They went unbeaten in 16 of 17 games to start the season. On January 19, 1975, in

Montreal, against a powerful Canadiens team, the Kings won 6-3 to move into first place ahead of Montreal at the All-Star break.

The playoffs that season featured a best-of-three series in the first round. This was a ridiculous setup by the NHL, because it allowed a poor team to have a couple of good games and eliminate a superior team, and that was exactly what happened. The Kings, with 105 points, met the Toronto Maple Leafs, who had only 78 points.

The first game was played in L.A. on April 8, 1975, and the Kings won in overtime 3-2 on Mike Murphy's goal at 8:53. The next game was in Toronto two nights later, and the Maple Leafs won in overtime on a goal by Blaine Stoughton at 10:19.

Due to a scheduling conflict at the Forum in L.A.—and the fact that Kings owner Jack Kent Cooke refused to play an afternoon game—the two teams played the deciding game the next night in L.A. This meant playing in Toronto one night followed by a cross-country flight to L.A. for the deciding game that next night. The two teams had decided to stay in Toronto and fly to L.A. the day of the game, but at the last minute, Maple Leafs owner Harold Ballard chartered a plane for his team, and they flew to Los Angeles right after the game Thursday night.

The Kings, who were an older team, stayed in Toronto and flew the day of the game, arriving in L.A. about 1:30 p.m. on game day. That night, Toronto jumped to a 2-0 lead at the end of two periods. Don Kozak scored for the Kings in the third, and the Kings kept hitting Toronto goalie Gord McRae with shot after shot, many of which he didn't see, but the Kings couldn't get the tying goal.

I'll never forget, with 10 seconds left, looking down from our broadcast location, seeing Toronto owner Harold Ballard and his sidekick King Clancy hugging and jumping up and down in the aisle as they eliminated the heavily favored Kings.

It was such a disappointment after a tremendous season that Kings coach Bob Pulford left the building in tears. Pulford always maintained that, because the Kings had older players, either they should have scheduled the deciding game with some rest in between or the Kings should have had a chartered flight home to get more rest. Because of Cooke's stubbornness, the Kings' best season ever was wasted.

BOSTON '76

In the 1975-76 season the Kings finished with 85 points, good for second place in the Norris Division. In the playoffs, they eliminated Atlanta in the first round in two straight games in the best-of-three series. Then they met the Boston Bruins in the quarterfinals. Boston had a great season that year finishing with 113 points, first in the Adams Division.

Boston was a heavy favorite and shut out the Kings 4-0 in Game 1. In Game 2, Butch Goring scored 27 seconds into overtime to give the Kings a 3-2 win and send the series to L.A. tied at one win apiece. The teams split in L.A. and headed back to Boston tied 2-2.

The Kings had an off day on Patriots Day in Boston, the day of the famous Boston Marathon. The finish line on Boylston Street was near the Kings' hotel, and we watched in person as the winner came in about 2 p.m. Four hours later, showered and dressed for dinner, a group of us approached the marathon finish line and noted that some runners were still coming in. My broadcast partner, Dan Avey, walked two blocks down the Marathon route and, dressed in a suit and tie, ran toward the finish line holding arms up in triumph. Some spectators actually started applauding. Did they think this guy ran 26 miles in a suit and tie without breaking a sweat?

The Kings lost Game 5 in a 7-1 rout, and on April 22, back in Los Angeles, the Kings faced elimination. As the Kings came on the ice that night, the crowd gave the team a prolonged standing ovation, dismissing the 7-1 embarrassment. The ovation lasted so long that referee Andy Van Hellemond told the Kings to start the national anthem or he was going to drop the puck for the start of the game. Unbeknownst to Van Hellemond, or anyone else at the time, the cord for the on-ice microphone ran near the visitors dressing room; and Boston's Wayne Cashman had deliberately cut the microphone cord with his skates. The singer *couldn't* start the anthem.

Boston had a 3-1 lead at the end of two periods. The Kings' Mike Corrigan scored in the third period, and the Kings trailed by one goal. Late the period, Corrigan skated in front of Bruins goalie Gerry Cheevers while chasing a loose puck. Cheevers tripped him, but no penalty was called. As Corrigan was sliding on his stomach toward the corner and away from Cheevers, he got his stick on the puck and in a sweeping motion sent it toward the Boston net. It deflected off Cheevers' stick, surprising him, and into the net for the tying goal with 2:12 remaining. The call of that goal was among the worst of my career, because I was so incensed that Cheevers had escaped a penalty call. I shouted, "Cheevers trips Corrigan. No penalty. I don't believe … Score! Corrigan scores."

I doubt if anyone listening on radio knew exactly what had happened except that the Kings had scored.

In overtime, I saw something I had never seen before—or since for that matter. Late in the overtime, the Kings' Bob Murdoch passed to Bob Nevin, who gave the puck to Butch Goring. As Goring came across the Bruins' blue line, he cut to his left and let go a shot from the top of the slot that beat Cheevers low just inside the left post. The Kings had won 4-3 at 18:28 into overtime, the longest game in Kings history to that point.

Then came an unforgettable sight. The Kings streamed off the bench, hoisting Goring to their shoulders to carry him off the ice. That's the only time I've ever seen that in hockey. On the radio broadcast, I was describing the scene and shouting, "We're going back to Boston. We're going to Boston for Game 7."

At the same time, down near the Bruins locker room, Kings publicity director Mike Hope was in a confrontation with Wayne Cashman, who Hope discovered had deliberately cut the microphone cord. He confronted him, and during the argument, Cashman swung his stick at Hope. Security personnel had to separate them.

Before Game 7 in Boston, Leigh Montville, an outstanding writer for the *Boston Globe*, wrote a story titled, "Kings of the Living Dead." The Kings had been shut out twice and humiliated 7-1 in the series, and yet, as Montville wrote, "They stick their fingers over the side of the coffin each time the lid is about to close. Two weeks ago, the Kings were a curiosity in Boston, now it's time to be afraid of the L.A. Kings. Man should always be afraid of things that won't die."

Unfortunately, the Kings did "die" that night, being shut out for the third time in the series, 3-0, to lose the series four games to three.

EDMONTON '89

The 1989 playoffs for the Kings featured Wayne Gretzky's first playoff in a Kings uniform; the best ever playoff series by a King; intravenous fluids; one of the greatest goals in Kings history; a rare comeback; a telegram from a former United States president; a Ukrainian priest; and a guy named "Lucky Butt."

The Kings took on Gretzky's teammates from the previous year, the Edmonton Oilers. Game 1 opened in Los Angeles on April 5 with the temperature 105 degrees. Kings goaltender Kelly Hrudey had been hospitalized with the flu the day before the game. He stayed in the locker room as the backup goalie. Center John Tonelli had the flu and was so sick he couldn't even attend the game. Kings goalie Glenn Healy had just recovered from the flu and lost 14 pounds during the game. He needed intravenous fluids between periods, and the Oilers won 4-3.

Game 2 was the next night, and it was still 105 degrees in L.A. Hrudey played in goal that night but went back to the hospital right after the game for more IVs and did not fly with the team to Edmonton. He flew up the next day. Kings forward Chris Kontos, who had played only seven games that season and scored only two goals, scored a hat trick to lead the Kings to a 5-2 victory. He had played earlier that season in Switzerland and joined the Kings late in the season.

The Oilers then won both games in Edmonton to take a 3-1 lead in the series. Only five teams in the 73-year history of the NHL had ever come back after that type of deficit.

Game 5 was played in L.A. and former president Ronald Reagan sent the Kings a good luck telegram. As they say, desperate times call for desperate measures. A Ukrainian priest from Alpine, California, in San Diego County said he could help, so he was allowed to speak to the team in the locker room before the game. He provided some inspirational comments, but his parting words were, "Just beat the shit out of the Oilers."

A guy named "Lucky Butt," connected with the *Mark & Brian* radio show on KLOS-FM sat with his bare butt on the Forum ice to jinx the Oilers. In 1988, he had sat with his naked behind on the pitcher's mound in Oakland; and the Dodgers beat the Athletics to win the World Series.

Kontos scored the first goal of the game for the third time in five games. It was his sixth goal of the series, and the Kings won 4-2 but still trailed in the series 3-2 as they headed back to Edmonton. Game 6 in Edmonton featured another appearance by "Lucky Butt," and one of the great goals in Kings history. With the Oilers leading 1-0, Kings forward Mike Allison had the puck and fought his way into the right-wing corner with Edmonton defenseman Randy Gregg trying to stop him. Allison continued behind the net, still with Gregg on his back; and then he came around to the left wing and put a shot between the pads of Oilers goalie Grant Fuhr to tie the score. That tremendous effort and goal gave the Kings the momentum they needed, and they scored three times in the final period to win 4-1 and even the series.

The seventh and deciding game was in Los Angeles on April 15, and again "Lucky Butt" sat on the ice. Gretzky scored on the first shot of the game, and Kontos scored his eighth goal of the series to set a club record. It was his sixth power play goal of the series, which was an NHL record. I remember more of Kontos' goals bounced off his body than off his stick. Gretky scored a shorthanded empty-net goal with 1:35 remaining to seal the comeback in a 6-3 win. After the final buzzer, Gretzky skated near the Oilers bench and pumped his arms in what appeared to be a mocking gesture, but he claimed that was not his intention, that he was just celebrating.

The Kings had nothing left for the next series, however, and even "Lucky Butt" couldn't pull them through. They lost four games to none to the Calgary Flames, who went on to win their first Stanley Cup.

CALGARY '90

The 1990 Stanley Cup Playoffs featured one of the greatest goals I've ever seen. The Kings were underdogs to the Calgary Flames, who had won the Stanley Cup the previous season. To stack the odds against the Kings, Wayne Gretzky wasn't with the team as they arrived in Calgary—he was back in Los Angeles suffering from a lower-back strain. It was the first playoff game he had missed in his career.

The Kings split the two games in Calgary, winning 5-3 and losing 8-5. When the series switched to L.A., Gretzky was back in the lineup, and the Kings won 2-1 in overtime on a shorthanded goal by Tony Granato. At that time, he was only the fourth player in NHL playoff history to score a shorthanded goal in overtime.

The next game in Los Angeles on April 10 featured a scoring explosion and another NHL record by the Kings. Three Kings players—Dave Taylor, Tony Granato, Tomas Sandstrom—all recorded hat tricks in a 12-4 Kings victory. At one point in the game, that trio had nine goals on nine shots. The three hat tricks in one playoff game set a NHL record.

With the Kings in position to win the series on April 14, two memorable plays occurred as the teams battled into overtime. With 2:23 left in the overtime period, it appeared as if the Flames had won the game. Doug Gilmour shot the puck, which glanced off Kings goalie Kelly Hrudey's pads and appeared to go over the line. The goal judge turned on the red light, and television replays indicated that the puck was in, but referee Denis Morel said he had lost sight of the puck and blown the play dead before the score.

The game continued into the second overtime, and at 3:14 the Kings won on an amazing goal by Mike Krushelnyski. Steve Duchesne shot from the right circle, Calgary goalie Mike Vernon made the save, but the rebound came right up the slot. Krushelnyski had been knocked down, but while lying on his back on the ice and a Calgary player on top of him; he somehow reached out to his left with one hand on his stick and flipped the puck in the air. Vernon, who was not a tall goaltender, was on his knees, and everything seemed to be in slow motion as he reached up, but the puck floated inches above his glove and into the net. Thus ended the longest game in Kings history—for the second year in a row, the Kings had eliminated the defending Stanley Cup champions. That was the end of the Kings' excitement, however, as they lost the next round to Edmonton in four straight games.

TORONTO '93

Kings fans had waited 26 years to embrace hockey the way they did in 1993. Actually, the 1992-93 season was a mediocre one for the Kings and held no promise of what was to unfold in the playoffs. Wayne Gretzky missed the first 39 games of the season with a herniated thoracic disk and didn't play a game until January 6, 1993. The Kings finished third in the Smythe Division and started each playoff series on the road. When the playoffs began the Kings won a high-scoring series against the Calgary Flames. With the series tied at two games apiece, the Kings scored nine goals in each of the next two games to win the series 4-2.

The next series opened in Vancouver against the Canucks and Game 5 featured the longest game in Kings history. Gary Shuchuk scored 6:31 into the second overtime to give the Kings a 4-3 win and a 3-2 lead in the series. Gerald Diduck had knocked Shuchuk woozy in the third period with a body check. Shuchuk went to the dressing room but returned later to score the game-winning goal. The Kings won the series 4-2 and moved past the second round for the first time in team history.

Then came the most memorable series I had ever been associated with—the Western Conference finals between the Kings and Toronto Maple Leafs. By this time, enthusiasm for Kings hockey was steadily building. Never before had I seen so many newspaper and television reporters on the road with the team. There were eight newspaper writers and five Los Angeles television stations in Toronto when the series opened on May 17.

In Toronto, we usually did our telecast from what they call "the broadcast gondola." It's located on the same level as the luxury suites. I arrived upstairs at about 6:15 and was shocked when Jim Fox met me and said, "I'm not working tonight." I asked why and he said, "Have you seen where they have us located?" I said I hadn't, and he said to follow him. We went up some stairs to a narrow catwalk above the main broadcast level and made our way to a makeshift booth some 100 feet above the ice. Jim is not too fond of heights, and the "booth" consisted of a counter and no walls. I walked to the counter, took it in both hands and tried to move it but it was solid. I mentioned that to Jim, but he said, "It may be solid now, but what about with 18,000 people jumping up and down in the building?"

Our Toronto television crew told Jim they would get him a safety belt and wrap it around one of the building's girders— that Detroit announcer Mickey Redmond had used one in the previous series. Jim agreed but said he wanted no mention of it on our telecast. After the first period, Jim realized our booth was not going to fall onto the ice, and he was fine the rest of the series.

Toronto won Game 1 but not before some fireworks. Toronto's Doug Gilmour had two goals and two assists, and with 2:34 left in the game, he was elbowed in the head by Kings defenseman Marty McSorley. Toronto captain Wendell Clark then fought with McSorley. Toronto coach Pat Burns was incensed and tried to get at the Kings bench after coach Barry Melrose. Burns told Melrose, who had shoulder-length hair, to get a haircut. Burns, who was quite heavy, was upset because Melrose puffed out his cheeks indicating Burns was fat. Later, when speaking of the confrontation, Melrose said he thought Burns was just ordering another hot dog. McSorley was so hated in Toronto that he said when he returned to his hotel after that game, his brother had cleaned up the messages on his voicemail. Marty said there were 102 messages, and 96 of them were threats.

The Kings won Game 2, 3-2, but the bad blood continued. With 2:43 left in the first period, McSorley hit Gilmour on the chin with a punch, but referee Don Koharski didn't see it. A few minutes later, McSorley and Gilmour got into a shoving match, and Gilmour head butted McSorley, but he got only a two-minute roughing penalty instead of the major penalty and game misconduct he should have received.

When the series moved to Los Angeles, the teams split, tying the series at two games apiece. The Leafs won Game 5 at home to take a 3-2 series lead and wanted to wrap up the series in Los Angeles, but Wayne Gretzky had other ideas. After the Maple Leafs' Game 5 win, Toronto newspaper writer Bob McKenzie wrote, "Gretzky is playing as if he's got a piano on his back."

There is a saying, "You don't tug on Superman's cape." After the pregame meal before Game 6, Gretzky told his agent, Michael Barnett, "The piano man still has a tune to play."

This is where the captains of both teams—Gretzky of the Kings and Wendell Clark of Toronto—rose to the occasion almost as if it were a Hollywood script. Clark, who had battled injuries throughout his career, scored the hat trick in Game 6, his third goal of the game coming with only 1:21 left in regulation to tie the score. Early in overtime, the Kings escaped a critical situation when Gilmour claimed he was high-sticked by Gretzky. The television replay did confirm that Gretzky's stick found Gilmour's chin and cut him, but neither the referee Kerry Fraser nor the linesmen saw the infraction. Even though Gilmour was bleeding, no penalty was called. Then, to add insult to injury, Gretzky scored 1:41 into the extra session to give the Kings the win and send the series back to Toronto for Game 7.

That final, deciding game, on May 29, was one of the greatest games I've ever had the pleasure of calling. There was so much tension knowing the Kings were one win away from going to the Stanley Cup Finals for the first time ever.

Gretzky said as he was going down in the hotel elevator to go to Game 7, he made small talk with a security guard about how crazy all the hype had been in the series. The guard told Gretzky that it wasn't very busy right at that time because the craziness would begin at 10:30 that night.

Gretzky was thinking, "Wow, this guys thinks Toronto is going to win, and it's going to be chaos here," so he told the guard,
"Don't worry about your job tonight at 10:30."

"Why not?" The guard asked.

"Because my job starts at 7:30," answered Gretzky.

Late in the third period with the game tied 3-3, the Kings
scored twice in 37 seconds to take the lead. Mike Donnelly
scored with 3:51 left and Gretzky with 3:14 remaining for his
third goal of the game. With about 2:15 left, the Kings' Dave
Taylor had a good chance on the right wing but missed wide on
a shot that would have given the Kings a 6-3 lead and put the
game away.

With only 1:07 left, Dave Ellett scored for Toronto to bring
them to within one goal. At this point, Kings coach Barry Melrose called a timeout, and he asked Pat Conacher, Dave Taylor,
and Wayne Gretzky to go back on the ice when the break ended.
Wayne said he turned to his coach and said, "I can't go. I've
played the last three-and-a-half minutes of the last four-and-a-
half minutes. I need a break." Gretzky later said, "That's the first
and only time I've ever done that in my career."

The last minute of the game was truly hectic both on the ice
and in the broadcast booth. I was sweating and became so nervous that several times I had to tell myself to settle down and just
call the game—not to get involved like a fan, because I had a job
to do. The final 50 seconds were spent in the Kings zone with
the Leafs buzzing all around the Kings net with an extra attacker.
I had the strangest feeling for about five seconds. A shiver came
over my body, and I felt as if I wouldn't be able to speak. If I
did say anything, it would be, "Don't let them score," which was
hardly something you would want to hear from a professional
announcer. With five seconds left, the puck was cleared to center ice; and on our telecast, I screamed, "THE KINGS ARE GOING
TO THE STANLEY CUP FINALS. THE KINGS ARE FOUR WINS AWAY
FROM THE STANLEY CUP." Several Kings fans told me later they

recorded those words and used them on their phone answering machines.

Gretzky has said this about that Game 7: "It was such a big game against a team and a city—and basically a country. That's why I often say it was the best game I ever played in the NHL. Now, did I have better games? Probably. But in that situation, Game 7 on the road, that was the most fun I ever had."

In Los Angeles, fans were going crazy. I heard from people who said, on many streets in the South Bay area of L.A. and the Pacific Coast Highway, you could hear horns honking; and in the restaurants and bars fans were screaming and cheering. I remembered thinking that many years ago no one believed that L.A. would ever be turned on to hockey that way. I called my wife, Judy, at home, and she had invited a couple of friends, Dona and Randy, over to watch the game. I talked with Randy and asked, "What are you doing?" and he said, "I'm jumping up and down on your furniture."

The only disappointing part was, we weren't in L.A. to join in the celebration. We went right to Montreal the next day for the start of the finals.

1993 STANLEY CUP FINALS

The Kings were a euphoric bunch as they headed to the Stanley Cup Finals in 1993. It was almost as if they didn't grasp the seriousness of the situation. The Montreal Canadiens had won 23 Stanley Cups in their storied history, and a press conference was held separately for each team at a Montreal hotel the day before Game 1. The Canadiens were the favored team, but they seemed to be uptight and serious when their coaches and some players met the press. When they were finished, the Kings came into the room, and I'll never forget how loose they seemed. At the head table sat Owner Bruce McNall, Coach Barry Melrose, and players Luc Robitaille, Wayne Gretzky, and Marty McSorley, all laughing and joking. The Montreal press was looking at them as if to say, "Do these guys know this is the Stanley Cup Final, or do they think it's an All-Star game?"

Melrose had prepared his team this way. He told them in their first meeting at training camp that season, "If you're afraid to talk about winning the Stanley Cup, you'll never win it." So the Kings weren't afraid to talk about winning the cup or to have fun playing in the finals.

Shortly after we arrived in Montreal, I went to the press headquarters hotel to pick up my credentials. Coming back down to the lobby in the elevator a woman asked me, "What exactly is the Stanley Cup?" I was shocked—never in Montreal did I expect to be asked that question, and I started looking for Allan Funt because I was sure I was on *Candid Camera*. "Where are you from?" I asked, and she said, "I'm from the United Kingdom."

I explained to her that the Stanley Cup is the oldest trophy competed for by athletes in North America and that it was much like the World Cup in soccer, which I felt she would understand. Before the Finals begin in the cities competing, the Stanley Cup and all the other NHL trophies are put on display in a hotel for the public to view. As the elevator doors opened, there was the gleaming Stanley Cup on display, so she also had a visual answer to her question.

Game 1 of the finals was on June 1, and the Kings shocked everyone in Quebec by winning 4-1 on two goals by Robitaille and a goal and three assists by Gretzky.

Game 2 featured one of the biggest blunders in Stanley Cup history. The game was tied 1-1 at the end of the second period, and longtime Montreal broadcaster Dick Irvin said to me, "If the Kings win tonight, they'll sweep the series. The Canadiens will never recover." With 1:45 remaining in regulation and the Kings leading 2-1, the Montreal players were hanging their heads, looking like a defeated team. But then something—like nothing I have ever seen in sports—happened that turned the momentum in Montreal's favor.

At that moment, Montreal challenged the legality of the curve on the blade of Kings defenseman Marty McSorley's stick. I remember, when referee Kerry Fraser took McSorley's stick to the penalty box for a measurement, my partner Jim Fox shook his head. He knew the stick was illegal.

Coach Barry Melrose said, "I'll always remember when Luc [Robitaille] came back to the bench because he was over at the penalty box and I said, 'Was it over?' Luc started laughing and said, 'Oh, it ain't even close.'"

McSorley got a two-minute penalty for playing with an illegal stick. Montreal had a powerplay, and they pulled goaltender Patrick Roy in favor of an extra attacker and a six-on-four advantage. With 1:13 left, they tied the score on a goal by Eric Desjardins, his second of the game. When the puck went into the net, John LeClair of Montreal was standing in the crease in front of Kings goalie Kelly Hrudey. Kings defenseman Charlie Huddy pointed this out, noting that the goal should be disallowed because LeClair was not shoved into the crease. There was no video review of that type of infraction at that time, and referee Kerry Fraser let the goal stand.

The game went into overtime, and 51 seconds later Desjardins scored again—his third of the game—to give Montreal a 3-2 win to even the series. It was the first time in NHL history that a defenseman had scored a hat trick in the Stanley Cup Finals.

McSorley's stick infraction didn't cause the Kings to lose the series because Montreal still had to win three more games, but it changed momentum so drastically that, from that point on, the Kings never had a lead in any game the rest of the series. All these years later, one wonders why McSorley was using an illegal stick—after all he only scored 15 goals that year and in his career scored just 108 in 961 career NHL games. McSorley accepted the blame saying that it was a "mistake" and that he "wasn't avoiding responsibility."

I remember how ecstatic Owner Bruce McNall was on the plane flight back to L.A. He was laughing and joking, and I thought, "Finally, this team is on solid footing and the future is bright." It was later revealed that he had to secure an emergency loan just to meet payroll. Nor did we know about legal problems that would put him in prison a few years later.

The first-ever Stanley Cup Final in Los Angeles was played on June 5, 1993. The Stanley Cup and other NHL trophies were on display at the Westin hotel and a steady stream of people, of all nationalities and colors, was arriving to view them and take pictures. The line started early in the morning and was still going late that night. Dick Irvin said, "I have never seen so many people lining up to see the Cup, not even in Montreal." It was another indication of how the Kings had captured the city.

Before the first game of the series in L.A., I did a live cut-in on our pregame show to comment on the atmosphere in the building. Just before we went on, I looked below our broadcast location and saw four season-ticket holders uncorking a bottle of champagne. They raised their glasses in a toast to something they probably thought they'd never see—a Stanley Cup Final in Los Angeles. I also remember the excitement and electricity in the building as they paraded the Cup out to center ice prior to the player introductions.

The celebration quickly subsided however, as Montreal took a 3-0 lead in the second period. Momentum then took a turn when Kings defenseman Mark Hardy threw a vicious check at Montreal's Mike Keane and dislodged a pane of glass. The Kings then scored three unanswered goals by Robitaille, Granato, and Gretzky to tie the score.

In sudden-death overtime, during a goal-mouth scramble, Montreal's John LeClair had three straight shots and scored the game-winning goal on the third shot. It was Montreal's ninth-consecutive overtime win that playoff year and gave them a 2-1 series lead.

The next game in L.A. followed the same pattern. The Kings trailed 2-0 in the second period when Mike Donnelly and Marty McSorley scored to tie the game. Again, for the third straight time, the teams battled into overtime. The Kings had eight of the first nine shots in the extra period; and Jimmy Carson hit the goalpost. For the second straight time however, John LeClair won the game for Montreal as he banked a shot off Kings defenseman Darryl Sydor, who was sliding toward the net to help goalie Kelly Hrudey. Incredibly, it was the tenth consecutive overtime victory for Montreal—a NHL-playoff record—and they led the 3-1 heading back to Montreal.

The final game was played on June 9, and Montreal beat the Kings 4-1 to win their 24th Stanley Cup, one of which came in 1916 before the National Hockey League was founded. At the end of the game, Gretzky hinted to the press that he might retire, and Montreal coach Jacques Demers asked Gretzky for his stick as a souvenir. He should've asked for McSorley's, too. I've also heard that the gauge used to measure the illegal stick was autographed by Coach Demers and Referee Fraser; and currently belongs to a sports-memorabilia collector living on Long Island, New York.

As the Kings boarded their bus for a trip to the airport, unruly Montreal fans started rocking and pounding the bus, beating on the windows with their fists, and they tore off the driver's-side mirror. It was suggested that we all move to the center aisle in case any of the windows were broken. Later on Montreal's St. Catherine Street, some $2 million worth of damage was done due to vandalism and looting.

I was wondering what would have happened if the Kings had won. About losing in those finals to Montreal, Gretzky has said, "I'll say this until I die—it was the most disappointing year of my life that we didn't win. Yet, it was the most rewarding year

I've ever had in my career because there were 22 players who believed in a coach and a system; who played hard, played together as a team, were unselfish. I had more fun maybe getting to the Stanley Cup Finals than I've ever had in hockey, and it's something I'll never forget."

That Finals series produced an all-time record for cable television ratings with a 22-percent share of the audience at one time. In fact, in the overtime of Game 4, more people in the Los Angeles area were tuned to Kings hockey than any other program on television at that time. Peak viewership in that game topped 725,000 homes and a 14.6 rating. There were more first-time hockey viewers than at any point in Kings history.

STUNNER AT STAPLES

The 1982 Kings playoff series with Edmonton featured the "Miracle on Manchester." In 2001—in their new building, Staples Center—the Kings had a playoff series with Detroit, which featured the "Fantasy on Figueroa" or the "Stunner at Staples."

That season the Kings finished third in the Pacific Division with 92 points and met the Detroit Red Wings in the first round. The Red Wings were heavily favored since they had piled up 111 points in the regular season, second best in the NHL. The series opened at Detroit, where the Kings lost both games 5-3 and 4-0, and it looked as if it would be an easy series for the Wings. As the series shifted to Los Angeles, the Kings won both games, 2-1 and 4-3.

The 4-3 win came in overtime on April 18, 2001. Detroit had jumped out to a 3-0 lead after two periods. Sometimes in a game, a team can be losing but creating enough scoring chances that you feel they may be able to rally and win. Such was not the case on this night. Well into the final period, Detroit was completely controlling the game.

With only 5:14 left in regulation, little-used forward Scott Thomas scored his first-ever playoff goal to get the Kings on the board. Thomas was only playing because Steve Kelly had taken ill with the flu before the game. Thomas had played only 24 games that season and scored just three goals.

With 3:22 left, Coach Andy Murray gambled and pulled goaltender Felix Potvin for an extra attacker. That left the Kings net wide open. With 2:27 left, Josef Stumpel scored a power-play goal, and the Kings trailed 3-2. Again, Potvin was pulled; and with 53 seconds left, Bryan Smolinski, skating to his right, fired from the right face-off circle and beat Detroit goalie Chris Osgood to tie the score.

The 18,478 fans, many of them wearing the red and white of Detroit, were on hand tying the all-time-record crowd ever to see hockey in California. Kings fans went wild— they had just witnessed the Kings score three goals in 5:14 to come from nowhere to send the game into overtime.

Another first occurred at 2:36 into overtime. Kings winger Adam Deadmarsh, on the right-wing boards near the corner, passed to Ian Laperriere at the right side of the Detroit net. He tipped it to his left to Eric Belanger, who had just jumped onto the ice, and Belanger ripped a shot under the crossbar for his first-ever playoff goal, the game-winner. Belanger was stunned for a moment, unsure if the puck had gone in or hit the crossbar. By this time his teammates were celebrating, as the Kings had snatched victory from what looked like a sure defeat.

The Kings then won the next game at Detroit to take a 3-2 lead in series and headed home to California to wrap it up on April 23.

The Kings trailed that night 2-1 entering the third period, but at 10:17, Deadmarsh tied the score and again the game went into overtime. At 4:48 of overtime, Deadmarsh scored on a rebound; the crowd went wild; and the Kings had won four straight over the mighty Red Wings to advance in the playoffs.

In the next round, the Kings met the Colorado Avalanche. With Colorado leading the series 3-1, the Kings won two straight 1-0 games behind outstanding shutout goaltending by Felix "The Cat" Potvin to force a seventh and deciding game in Denver. In that game, the Avalanche scored four goals in the third period to win 5-1, eliminating the Kings. They eventually went on to win the Stanley Cup.

AFTERWORD

HALL OF FAME

One morning in June 2000, I received a phone call from Chuck Kaiton, the president of the NHL Broadcasters Association. "Congratulations," he said, "you've been voted in to the Hockey Hall of Fame."

I couldn't believe it. Chuck told me I would receive the Foster Hewitt Memorial Award, which goes to radio-television broadcasters who have made outstanding contributions to the profession and to the game during their career in hockey broadcasting. Selected by the NHL Broadcasters Association, the honoree receives a plaque in the Hockey Hall of Fame in Toronto, Ontario, Canada.

The induction took place in Toronto on November 13, 2000, and my wife, Judy; our daughter, Kristin, and her husband, Gilbert; and our son, Kevin, were there with me. I was honored when numerous colleagues and friends from around the country attended as well.

Bob Miller with his family at the Hockey Hall of Fame induction ceremony, November 2000. From left: his son-in-law, Gilbert Gonzaga, his daughter, Kristin, Bob Miller, his wife, Judy, and his son, Kevin. *PHOTO PROVIDED BY BOB MILLER*

In my speech during the plaque presentation, I acknowledged those people who had a profound impact on my career: my mother, who worked two jobs after my father passed away so I would have the opportunity for a college education; my wife and children, who are hockey fans and gave me full support in my vocation even though I was away from home on many nights; and my on-air partners, the Kings owners, coaches, and players.

In that speech, I mentioned that I don't feel anyone—including players—ever start their career thinking of being in the Hall of Fame. Thus, when it happens, it is a tremendous feeling of accomplishment. I said I was most proud of my longevity with one team, the Los Angeles Kings. As of this writing, it's been 33 years. These days, when so few people desire to make a commitment—or in this business when so many people make a big splash for a while and then disappear—I am extremely proud that I have been with one team for such a long period of time.

That's what the Hall of Fame means to me. Longevity, recognition of a commitment, and lasting fame that will be visible for all to see now and forever more.

Bob Miller delivers his acceptance speech at the Hockey Hall of Fame induction in November 2000. *PHOTO PROVIDED BY BOB MILLER*

HOLLYWOOD WALK OF FAME

People all over the world have heard of the famous Hollywood Boulevard Walk of Fame. It is one of the most visited attractions in Los Angeles, and each year hundreds of thousands of tourists and local citizens walk the Boulevard to see the names of the stars embedded in the sidewalk. Names representing the fields of motion pictures, music, live stage performances, radio, and television.

On Monday, October 2, 2006 I was extremely pleased to be included among those honored. The ceremony took place at the exact location where the star is placed, and hundreds of relatives, friends and Kings fans attended. Fox Sports West televised the festivities live.

My sister and brother-in-law, Bev and John Samuelson of Elkhorn, Wisconsin, arrived several days before the ceremony. Bev said she wanted to see the Walk of Fame, so we drove there on Friday afternoon. We discovered that the actual tile with my star was covered with plastic and surrounded by wooden barriers. Bev said she wanted a photo of me at the location. As usual, many people were walking by as I posed for the photo, and a woman and her adult daughter stopped right next to me and the woman said, "I wonder whose star this is," but I didn't respond. They talked a little longer, and again the woman said, "Yes, I wonder whose star this is," and this time I turned to her and said, "It's my star." She looked at me and said in a sarcastic manner, "Yeah, right" and walked away. It was a very comical moment and gave me something to repeat in my speech when the actual ceremony took place. I can just imagine the shock on their faces if they were watching the live telecast three days later.

Author Bob Miller stands beside his star on the Hollywood Walk of Fame. *PHOTO BY KEVIN MILLER*

CPSIA information can be obtained
at www.ICGtesting.com
Printed in the USA
LVOW08*0008271216

518781LV00018B/419/P